Flobird
A Bird's Eye View

by
Cherie Johnson

 Maximilian Press Publishers
920 S. Battlefield Blvd., suite 100
Chesapeake, Virginia 23322
757-482-2273

Copyright © 2005 Cherie Johnson
All rights reserved,
Including the right of reproduction
In whole or in part in any form.

MAXIMILIAN PRESS PUBLISHERS and colophon
are registered trademarks of
Maximilian Press Publishing Company

Author Cherie Johnson

Cover Design by John Walker

Manufactured in the United States of America

10 9 8 7 6 5 4 3 2 1

ISBN: 1-930211-67-8

Paper used in this publication meets the minimum
requirements of ANSI/NISO Z39.48-1992 (1997)
(PERMANENCE OF PAPER)

DEDICATION

This book is dedicated
to all the *birds with broken wings*
who have learned to fly again
because of the entity
known as Flobird.
May you and those you touch
continue to fly high
on the wings of God's love.

Thank You

Mom for living - for without you and your experiences, there would have been little to say; Marchand for just being there; Jim for being my partner in life during this writing and supporting me in all my endeavors, and to everyone who helped to bring this book to fruition. Thank you for your patience, your support, your input, for making it possible to reach out and touch others with the wisdom, sorrow, love, and joy that made up Flobird, the Seagull.

Contents

Introduction by Dalton Roberts
Flobird The Seagull song by Doug Allmen

1 The Beginning 1
2 Flobird's Eye View 41
3 Meeting Flobird 79
4 How Flobird Affected Lives 89
5 Likes and Dislikes 107
6 Traveling With Flobird 113
7 Dying 127
8 Return To The Enchanted Forest 139
9 The Funeral 147
10 The Here and Now 155

Pictures 165

Cherie Johnson's striking book about the life of her mother is much more than a daughter's loving tribute. It is an insightful, in-depth look into one of the most unusual lives ever lived on this planet. Flobird was much more than one-of-a-kind. She was one unlike all other kinds we have ever heard or read about.

My acquaintance with Cherie began when I read a brief article she wrote about Flobird's life for Science of Mind Magazine. It instantly became essential that I know the author better and find out more about her unbelievable mother. When she left Hawaii and came back to the continental states for a visit, I arranged to meet her.

That visit and an editorial review of her Flobird manuscript convinced me that Flobird is real.

Trying to write about a person so rare and unusual runs the risk of disbelief. We have trouble believing people so unlike us can exist. We have so many tidy little mental filing nooks for people that we are unprepared for a Flobird.

For that matter, we are unprepared for a Cherie. Those who can see the splendor of a life like Flobird's are a rarity. She not only saw that splendor, she has been able to transform her own life through accessing the awesome spiritual energy that powered Flobird. She lives the same spiritual principles and possesses an uncanny ability to transmit them to others. I have decided this skill comes from a deep knowing of the truths behind the energy.

All who read this book will never be the same. They will forever know there are dimensions of consciousness beyond anything they have lived or seen. They will know it is possible for us to live this Earth-life as spiritual beings.

Dalton Roberts
Columnist and author of
Things That Really Matter
and Kickstarts

FLOBIRD THE SEAGULL
Written by Doug Allmen

Flobird the Seagull
Flobird with Love
Flobird with happiness
Flying in the sun.

CHORUS:
Flobird, Flobird, flying in the sun
You have taught me happiness
Never more shall I cry.

Before you came into my life I felt that I must die.
You wrapped me in your golden wings and took me to the sky.
I walked upon a gloomy path where naught but hate was true.
Then God took me to His arms and delivered me to you.

CHORUS

Oh God, I cried, what shall I do? My life has been so wrong,
So empty and filled with pain, I shall end it for long.
A life of illusion - a life of make believe -
Then you opened up my eyes and showed yourself to me.
A natural life, a natural high, this is the way indeed.
A life of phoniness is not for you or me.

CHORUS

Down upon the beach she lay her body wracked with pain.
The seagulls flew above her head...and then she smiled again.
And then she turned and took my heart and chased away my fear.
Flobird said a few kind words, and I knew God's love was here.

Flobird, Flobird, of these words I'm sure
Flobird is God herself, purest of the pure.

(The Author)

FLOBIRD:
A Bird's Eye View
by
Cherie Johnson

The true story of Florence Joan Martin who after searching for 'highs', was brought to her knees by alcoholism. With her introduction to the 12 Steps of AA in 1960, and given just 6 months to live, she changed her name to "Flobird" traveled the world for the next 18 years on an amazing spiritual journey that touched hundreds of "1st & 2nd Generation Birds" who still carry her message today. Told through Flobird's own words, through the accounts of many of her contemporaries, and compiled by her daughter, Cherie Johnson, this is one story that will touch your curious soul.

Author, Cherie Johnson, currently resides in central Florida where she is working on a follow-up book, "Feathers", and can be reached at:
DanceDivaOnline@yahoo.com

THE BEGINNING

To live each day, one day at a time, have an open heart and open hands.

-- Flobird

CHERIE

Turning within to the Spirit and daring to "follow your heart" (the inner urging) is not an easy assignment. But I was blessed to have a great teacher in my life. She was like a Cosmic Hobo who dared to go anywhere her inner feelings told her, no matter how illogical or humanly impossible it seemed. She taught me to trust my own inner feelings and not worry about the outcome. Her name was Florence Joan Johnson, and she was my mother.

I was fifteen years old the first time I experienced what it meant to follow my heart. Flo had just come home from the doctor after being told she only had six months to live. The doctor said that among other things, she had a cirrhotic liver, only one functioning kidney, and gallstones. This physical condition was due primarily to her alcoholism.

Flo had always loved life, but seldom herself. She was a risk taker, loved to play poker, and bet on the horses at Caleinte. Drinking went hand in hand with her life style. It was her panacea.

She was the middle daughter of three, looking for approval from her big Sis, Lorraine, and feeling protective towards Vivian, her younger sister. She became estranged from her family in her late thirties and did not speak to or see her mom and step-dad for thirty years. Even at her death, she did not want to contact either of her sisters.

She was filled with conflicting ideas and emotions, seemingly torn between two worlds. But with alcohol, she was free of any fear of what others thought of her and free of what she thought of herself. Flobird's favorite song, and her theme in life was Don't Fence Me In. She would sing it while cleaning house or driving. Without the alcohol, she was trapped - in herself, in her life, in her fear. With alcohol, life was an adventure, and she didn't need to worry about the outcome.

She became a daily drinker, using alcohol as her cure-all, until, at the age of forty-two, a golfing buddy led her to Alcoholics Anonymous.

Even in her drinking, Flo read and studied spiritual teachers like Emmet Fox, Ernest Holmes, and Joel S. Goldsmith, and was a long-time subscriber to Science of Mind magazine. These books became her friends. They told her there was more to life than meets the eye, but because of her low self-esteem, she believed these things happened to others - not her. After joining AA and finding sobriety, she soon discovered that she too, could experience the life she had been reading about.

So, after hearing the doctor's prognosis that day, Flo went home, flipped open the Bible to the passage, "...leave Mother, Father, Sister, Brother and follow me...," called the lawyer who was handling her divorce and instructed him to give everything to her husband, then packed her clothes. She was determined to take the time she had left on this earth and experience what she had been reading about.

One book she had read mentioned turning "stones into bread." Having little money, she looked around to see what "stones" she might have. Flo's golf clubs and some bricks she found lying around the house were sold, and she was ready to try this life of faith. After all, she had nothing to lose. I was on summer break, and was invited to come along (my younger sister was living with our dad).

We packed the car with what she had determined was necessary and headed for the freeway. At the entrance, Flo turned to me and asked, "Which way should we go?" I chose South. So, off we went, South on Interstate 5.

When we ran out of road, we found ourselves in Imperial Beach, California, just five miles north of Tijuana. I was there for only a few days because some friends in San Diego had heard we were there, came to see us and took me back to San Diego with them.

Not unlike Noah and his Ark, Flo spent forty days and nights on the sand dunes of Imperial Beach. She built a house from items the ocean washed ashore. Walls were made of crates; an old tire served as a chair; the roof was the sky and stars above. One morning in answer to her query, "Ocean, ocean, what did you bring me?" she found a small refrigerator to keep her food in. She spent her days in quiet contemplation, studying her spiritual books.

When someone wandered into her domain, she offered coffee and food (usually a peanut butter sandwich), and shared her experience. Fisherman often brought her lobster and cooked it for her. Others would bring her cigarettes. Her needs were always met.

When I returned a few weeks later, she told me this story. "I awoke one morning as usual, the sun caressing my face. But instead of feeling the joy of being alive and gratitude for being sober, I found myself obsessed with alcohol. My mind, body, and soul wanted to drink. I had been passing kidney stones and was in a lot of pain; I had liver spots on my nose, and when I looked at myself in a mirror, I saw a witch. I looked to the ocean, and it became a sea of vodka. Running toward it, I fell over a sand dune and began to crawl. As I neared the ocean, I became aware of a flock of seagulls overhead and turned over to look at them.

"Suddenly the sky, ocean and sand melted into one and turned to pure white light. A vision came to me that all life was pure light changing form. I saw humanity as little expressions of God running around. I knew at that moment there was no time or space, that life was just an illusion and everything was perfect in its changing form -- that love was man's true nature, and all of life was a divine comedy.

"When I sat up, I realized the craving for alcohol was gone."

We returned to Riverside, California, and Flo told everyone, "We're just one big glob of God. Look to the air and watch the birds. They neither sow, nor reap, nor gather into barns, their heavenly Father watches over them. You, too, can be a bird!" Most people thought she was crazy; a few listened. She became known as Flobird. Florence Joan had died on a sand dune.

For the next eighteen years, Flobird beachcombed the world, defying the doctor's prediction of death. By "following her heart" as she called it, she traveled to Europe, the Middle East, and all corners of the United States. There was always someone at her destination who was helped by what she had to share.

One morning, when she was employed as the Administrator of a Halfway House in Sunset Beach on the north shore of the island of Oahu in Hawaii (a Halfway House is a place where drug addicts and alcoholics can go to get clean and sober), Flobird was "called" by her inner urging to go to the beach. She had to wake up a couple of the addicts staying there in order to get her car started, and when she arrived to stand at the ocean's edge, she felt, rather than heard, something behind her. As she turned, a dirty, scraggly, skinny form of a man crawled out from under a bush and stammered, "Are you F-f-flo-b-bird?" She said, "Yes, honey. You must be what I came here for."

Flobird took him back to the Halfway House, and through her love, caring, and sharing, he let go of drugs and alcohol and has never returned to them.

Two years later, several of us were camping on the Big Island of Hawaii. Flobird came out of her tent and announced, "Little Boss (her name for Jesus) just told me to go to Egypt by boat. Anyone wanna come?" "Sure," several of us answered, "we're not doing anything else." That was the beginning of a two year journey across the states, Europe and the Middle East. We did go to Egypt by boat, and were led to Cairo where we met a man who had been off alcohol for a year by himself, and was praying for someone to help him.

Whenever Flobird got a prepare to leave this place message, we never knew where the money (or green energy as she referred to it) would come from. Sometimes we'd turn stones into bread by selling items we had, and sometimes money would come in from unexpected sources. But there was always enough to do what we needed to do.

You could find Flobird most often sitting on the beach facing the ocean, clad in a brightly-colored hand-made bikini, her gray-streaked brown hair hanging freely down the middle of her back, a cigarette holder held lightly in her right hand, smeared with Love That Red lipstick and filled with a Camel which burned incessantly. She gave an appearance of great height and strength, but she felt small and fragile when you hugged her. She referred to her 5'8" large-boned, thin-skinned frame as her bag of bones. Her face was dotted with freckles from the sun and deeply etched with lines that she called her character wrinkles. She let her waist-length hair hang free except for the top section which she wore in a braid on top of her head. Her hazel eyes sparkled with light when she smiled, and her mouth spread from ear to ear. She seemed ageless, and you felt she was the most beautiful woman alive.

It was not uncommon for a complete stranger to be drawn to her and end up listening intently as she shared her life's experiences. Flobird spoke the language of love and people gravitated to her like to a magnet, especially young people who were dying on the vine of life from drugs and alcohol.

The following is from Tom, that dirty, scraggly, skinny form of a man that crawled out from under the bush that day at Sunset Beach:

Flobird. She was one of those rare people of whom legends are made. Of the people who knew her intimately and asked, you would hear a different perception from each one. All would agree though that she was a tremendously gifted person, and as open a channel of God's love as I have seen or experienced. She used to say something that would blow some people away. She'd say 'I am sure of God and God is sure of me.' Then she would go and live it.

In all the years I knew her, she never had any outer means of support. No income. She didn't work at a job, or collect welfare, or social security. She said she worked for God, and that God took care of her through His open channels. I've seen her live in beautiful mansions, in tents, and even in a cave in Israel, small little rooms, vans - it didn't really make much difference to her - she was excited and grateful for wherever she was. She said she gave up complaining - that it was all transitory anyway. Life was an adventure and that wherever God wanted to place her body, it was all right with her. Her purpose in this life was to be of love and service.

I asked her once what she thought God's will was for me,

and what she told me kicked off in me my conception of God. She said that God's will for me was to live, love, laugh and be happy for His sake. That I was an expression of God, and that it was selfish for me to be miserable because God wanted to enjoy his creation through me.

Physically, Flobird was a sick woman. Alcohol and drugs had destroyed her body. Sometimes she was in tremendous pain and would break down crying. I would try to comfort her, and she'd come up with this courage that was born of humility and say it was no big thing. That this too would pass. That if we were afflicted, it was for the good of others. I was always amazed by how quickly she would come out of her suffering. No medication. No doctor. Just God.

People would come to see her during these periods, and she'd sit and rap to them for hours. She had a spiritual dialogue that would flow endlessly. These people would leave inspired and high on life. When they were gone, Flobird would fall apart crying, racked with pain. And they never knew. I watched it for ten years. Believe me, she was consistent.

Every morning she'd wake up around 3:30 or 4:00 AM and meditate. It didn't matter if she was up all night with a sick addict, or a drunk, or not. She said she had a choiceless awareness, and that God chose her; she didn't choose Him. In meditation different things would come to her. Some of it was pretty esoteric. Sometimes she would say she was picking up on the suffering of mankind, or the selfishness of mankind.

There were always a bunch of us clean and sober addicts/alcoholics living with her. When she'd say God told her to go here or there, we'd go with her. She'd always tell us to follow our own hearts. I'm not too sure we knew what our hearts were telling us. We'd just go with her. Maybe that was what our hearts were saying.

I once called her my spiritual mother, and that's the last time I ever called her anything except Flobird. She turned and pointed her finger at me and said, "I am not Mother, Teacher, or Master. My name is Flobird, and I am a happy, grateful alcoholic and addict just like you, and don't you ever forget it!" I never did. And I'm sure grateful for it. Because by her example she kept me turned towards God.

I told her I wanted what she had. She said, "If you want what I have and are willing to go to any lengths to get it, then take the steps I took." She guaranteed I could have it.

She started a meeting called the Beachcombers Spiritual Progress Traveling group. And it literally traveled wherever she went.

I had been clean and sober for a few months. Flobird and a few other addict/alcoholics were living in tents on the Big Island of Hawaii. At first I felt rejection from not being able to live with them. But I see now, had I been there, my dependence surely would have been shifted over to Flobird instead of God.

One thing she threw at me over and over again was that love-in-action was the magic way. That I would change and grow in leaps and bounds if I surrendered my little self to love and service.

She was an able example. You could absolutely lose the "puny little self." She would work with people day in and day out, and that enthusiasm and love was never depleted. It seems there was a reservoir of river that she tapped into. It made me and others realize without a doubt that there was something greater happening here. It made you want to set your sights on being as open a channel as you could. Nothing else in life really was as important. If ever I was searching for meaning and purpose in life, I found it.

After awhile I went with her and the others traveling around the islands, living in the parks.

She got judged a lot by different AA members. Many resented her bringing all the drug addicts to meetings. A lot of them thought she was nuts and must be having sex with all these young guys. (She had been celibate all the time I knew her). At one time they even had an anti-Flobird meeting and wrote to the New York service office of Alcoholics Anonymous about her. New York responded by sighting the Fourth Tradition, that every group was autonomous.

She had a lot of contact with the General Service Office, and they used to encourage her to keep on doing what she was doing. As she would put it, to follow her heart.

Living with her was rough at times. Growing along spiritual lines was intensified. We couldn't get away with self pity. One time I had an ear infection. I was in a lot of pain, lying down on my mat in the tent, and whining and moaning in my typical addict style. She walked in, looked at me, and said, "Self pity will get you nowhere. Get off your ass and get into loving action." She pissed me off so bad that I got up, hating her guts. I washed the dishes in spite and hoped to die. But by the time I was finished with the dishes my ear stopped hurting. She told me afterwards that she couldn't believe she actually said that. She just walked into the tent and looked at me, and it came blurting out of her mouth.

She had a psychic ability that was maddening for us. She would know what we were thinking before we would tell her. She would tell us what we were gonna say before we would say it.

One time I was on one side of the island talking to a girl friend and suddenly, in the middle of our conversation I said, "Let's move back to the Mainland." I was aghast that I said that because the last thing I wanted to do was go back to California. That night I went to a meeting, and Flobird came in the door. I got up to give her a hug, and she pointed her finger at me and said, "You're going back to the Mainland." She said she was on the other side of the island talking to a friend when the words came out in the middle of her conversation that Tom is going back to the Mainland. I had no money and had no idea where I would stay if I went. But, in two weeks I was back in Venice, California, and a house was made available to me.

There were many experiences like that with her. Probably the most bizarre was when we were camping at Harry K. Brown Park on the Big Island. I didn't have a pillow and was gonna take a nap one afternoon. Flobird was gone somewhere. I went over to her side of the tent, took her pillow and went to sleep. I dreamed I was climbing a mountain. I got to a crevice and was trying to boost myself up when all of a sudden a dog came up from behind me and was trying to get up the mountain also. It got between my legs and was rubbing against me. It stimulated me enough to have an orgasm. I woke up and realized I'd had a wet dream. I interpreted the dream to mean that my animal instincts wanted to be expressed. I hadn't had any sex for almost a year. I put Flobird's pillow back and took off.

Later when I returned, I saw Flobird standing outside of the tent. She was looking straight at me. I noticed that her pillow and pillow case were hanging on the clothes line. As I walked up she said to me, "Did you sleep on my pillow?"

I said, "Yeah, why?"

And she said, "Did you dream about screwing a dog?"

I couldn't believe it. I said, "Yeah, I did."

She just shook her head and said, "Damn it. Don't use my pillow again. I was trying to meditate, and this thought of screwing a dog kept going across my head. I finally located the vibration from the pillow."

My reaction was, "Well, excuse me. I'll let you know which way I walk, so you won't have to cross my path."

It makes you kind of paranoid. This kind of stuff was spontaneous with her. She couldn't make it happen. It would just happen.

All of us would wake up early in the morning around 3:30 or 4:00 AM, go our separate ways, and meditate until sunrise. Sometimes I would come back to the tent to get some coffee, and I'd see Flobird meditating. She'd be gone somewhere deep within. We'd all get together afterwards and read from the books or just talk about life, God, love, the Fellowship of AA, and the message of recovery. She would say that the best part of her day was the quiet time she spent alone with God.

I know from experience that it was the alone time Flobird spent with God in prayer and meditation, and the love-in-action she did every day that allowed her the extra 15 years of life. But finally, at the age of sixty-one, Flobird's body was riddled with cancer; she weighed all of 112 pounds. Her body had been in great pain for over a year, but, as usual, she never complained. Instead she overcame the pain by constantly giving to others, sharing her experience, healing birds with broken

Flobird: A Bird's Eye View

wings and helping them to fly free once again.

Flobird died July 16, 1978, on a beloved piece of land in Grants, New Mexico. She has been my greatest teacher and inspiration.

What follows is her story as told by her in her own words, and a compilation of letter-tapes during the final four years of her life as well as experiences from the birds whose broken wings she was able to mend simply by sharing her experience, strength and hope.

FLOBIRD

My name is Flobird, and I am a happy, grateful alcoholic and drug addict, living today ONLY by the Grace of God in AA. And that's rigorous honesty. I of myself cannot do it. I used to wonder who Grace was. I found out it means gift.

I didn't know I was an alcoholic until they brought me to AA dead on the vine. I didn't even know we had AA. I just knew I was totally insane. Today I've accepted my spiritual insanity. It's so great. I get drunk on spiritual wine. People look at me with that strange look and say, "What are you on?"

But, let me tell you a little of what I used to be like, and what's happened and what I'm like today.

Well, let's see. At eight years old I turned my back on God. That's when I committed adultery. To me, that's what adultery is - turning our backs on God. I used to be so frightened because I committed adultery. Anyway, at eight years old, I had one little boyfriend in Phoenix, Arizona, and he died of a busted appendix. He fell dead in my lap. When I ran and got Mother, she came out and said, "Oh, God took him." As I looked at him, I asked, "Why?" "Well," she said, "God is a punishing God." So I connected God with taking everything that you ever loved.

My grandfather was a hard-shelled Baptist, and he told me all the time if I did wrong, I was going to Hell in Jesus' precious name -- and I was always doing wrong. That's where I shut the door on God and became an atheist.

When I turned my back on God, I felt rejected; I put the coffin on my back, and the death wish was born. I found this out in my 4th Step inventory.

I didn't want to live in this world from the time I was eight years old. That emotion of feeling unwanted, unloved, reoccurred in every facet of my life. This feeling of being isolated in a world of people that I could not relate to took root in me.

So I grew up with no God. I grew up as a rebel. You'd tell me I couldn't do something, I would show you, and I'd do it! I was called a juvenile delinquent and kicked out of school. I was incorrigible. I was one that ran from violence, and I ran from people that were dominating. I could never share the most inner self of me with anybody.

I suppressed my emotions. I used to love people that could tell people off because when I'd get angry, I'd go home and carry on the conversation with myself. "This is what I'll tell them when I meet them next." But the next time I'd see them, I'd do what they wanted me to do. I was a people pleaser.

At ten years old I remember lying in the clover in Arizona wondering what my purpose in life was. Why can't I die. I don't want to live. I found alcohol at 14. It became my strength. I could talk to people. I could tell them the things I felt inside.

Alcohol became my friend. I got such a wonderful feeling when I drank it. I loved the taste of it, the feel of it, and I could hardly do without it wherever I went. I even used to gargle it. This emptiness, this hole that was in my gut from a little child went away, and I knew there was some reason for me to be here. Alcohol was my reason.

I drank straight Canadian Club with a beer chaser. I could out drink anybody. They'd all pass out, and I'd go right on drinking. I was a loner. Just leave me with my drink. I could walk in any bar by myself and sit and drink, play music and cry. Just let me out of this world. I used to study medical books and philosophies trying to find out and understand what life was, to find the meaning of my own misery, and if there could be a God.

When I was 16, I fell in love for the first time. I didn't know what sex was, except on the evil side of it, so I used to peek in windows and watch people, and I thought it was horrible. My idea of sex was contempt, and yet, inside of me it was sacred.

If you got married, that was it. You never slept with another man.

So at 16 I told this to this fellow, and he told me we were going to get married. Then I found his little black book. It had a list of all the girls that he'd conquered. And there I was. He had written, "It took me a whole year to conquer her." When I read that, my heart cracked into many pieces.

It took me five years to marry him, and three months to leave him. Retaliation.

Since that time, I've been married seven times. It was, get 'em, reject 'em, leave 'em.

At that time I closed the door of my heart and started building emotional walls around it, so no one could get in. No one could hurt me. I built emotional and mental walls. I'll do it all myself. I don't need people. I don't need anything.

At 17 I was on skid row, and I became a Dime-A-Dance dancer. I was saved from prostitution, I see now, by a Higher Power. It didn't seem to be my thing. I was a bar drinker. I'd sit at the bar, but I'd pay for my own drinks. I knew if anybody paid for them, I'd have to go to bed with them. And that wasn't my bag. Then, one time in New York, I woke up, looked over, and said, "Who are you?"

It's a strange thing, how we try to protect ourselves because it just isn't right, then we black out and end up doing those things we didn't want to do anyway.

Somebody told me I looked like Joan Crawford, so I went to Hollywood to be her stand in, and I ended up on skid row. I always wanted to be somebody else. I didn't want to be me. I was always looking for me. I was seeking me through bottles. Books. Everything. When I was 18 I had a little knowledge about everything. Philosophy - I could quote Shakespeare, I could quote Confucius, but I couldn't tell you how to love, I couldn't tell you how to live. I could only say, "You can have anything you want in this world, if you don't hurt anybody by getting it. And stand on your own two feet. Don't ask anybody for help. Get 'em before they get you." And I did. In a subtle way. Now I see my suicide attempts were attention-getters, my own self-pity emerging, but I didn't know what these emotions were. I didn't know what thinking meant. I've read Norman Vincent Peale, Change Your Thinking. He told us to meditate, but I didn't know how to do it.

I had a contempt for money and became a gambler. I was a black jack dealer, and I played the horses for six years. Drinking and gambling. I loved it.

Then I decided I was gonna try to do something good. Give my life to my country, so I joined the Navy and became a radio operator. But I was a very drunk radio operator. As a radio operator, you have to drink in order to receive the codes (as least I thought so at the time), so I had a good excuse.

I was sent to Pensacola, Florida, and became a radio instructor. The old Chiefs used to give me all my rum, and warm Ponce de Leon beer - got awful drunk on that. I was so undisciplined. I wouldn't salute the 90-day wonders. I got Captain's Mast about every month. One day I was sitting at Bronson Field sending code when all of a sudden this urge came over me. I got up, went into town and started at the San Carlos bar. I had three shots of Canadian Club with beer chasers (my favorite drink), and from that time on I remember nothing else. It was a black out.

A week later I was lying in the hospital at Bronson Field, and Commander Bulwinkle and Peters were standing there saying, "I think she's dead. Let's put out the bulletin."

But I was alive. I remember lying there pickled in alcohol and unable to move. I was trying to wiggle my eye or something to let them know I was alive. It's a strange feeling to have someone say you're dead when you know you're alive. They started to walk out the door, and I don't know what I did, but I heard Commander Bulwinkle say, "Well, just a moment."

Three days later I came out of it. But I got a Deck Court. The psychiatrist and doctors, all these men of knowledge, were sittin' out there with this list of things that I had done. I had beat up a little ol' lady, I had hit a policeman over the head with his billy club (a great big guy - but drunk we can do anything). The list went on and on. The psychiatrist kept watching me as they read the list to me. He asked, "Don't you feel guilty?" I said, "No, sir, I didn't do those things. I didn't do 'em." And I started crying. I sat there not guilty because I didn't remember it. I had blacked out.

They called it toxic amnesia. (When I first came to AA, they asked me if I'd ever blacked out, and I said, No, never did. But once somebody said I had toxic amnesia. And one of my sponsors said, "Baby, that's a blackout." I also never got drunk. I got intoxicated. I really hated the word drunk. The good doctors couldn't understand. They busted me to RN 1. My commanding officer asked me if I wanted out of the Navy. I said, "Yes." So they gave me an undesirable discharge.

I knew I was totally insane when they kicked me out. They tore my patches off my uniform, and I felt completely disgraced, and humiliated. You see, my big Sis was a Major in the Army Air Corp. She tried to make a lady out of me all of her life by sending me to places like charm school, but I'd go get drunk and disappoint her. I tried to prove to her I was a good girl, but I couldn't do it. And I had failed her again. (She got out of the Army as a Major, drinking heavily, but informing me she's not an alcoholic. However, alcoholism led to her death.)

I got out of the Navy, and went to work for the railroad. There's another place I drank myself to death. I had to receive code from the railroad and hand up orders as the trains went by. As I look back I see it was by the Grace of God that I never started main line meets.

In my 30's the body started disintegrating, but I was so happy they found something wrong with the body. I knew something was wrong, and I'd go to the doctors, and they said I had neurasthenia. They sent me to Patten State Hospital for three months. My face was paralyzed. The doctor called me a manic depressive 'cause I couldn't stop crying. He asked, "Why are you crying, why can't you stop?" I said, "All these poor people here." He said, "You're the one I'm sorry for. You have conscious contact. They're happy. They're doing what they want to. They have a bed. They have food, and we take care of them." They labeled me many things including paranoid, and schizophrenic, but not alcoholic.

They were going to give me shock treatment. I said, "I don't want you to fool with my head!" It was in 1950 and everyone was afraid of mental illness, so I couldn't tell anybody I'd been in the mental institution 'cause if I did, they'd run from me. There was such a fear of mental illness. Of course the fear of mental illness is still very prominent now, but then, it was something you just didn't talk about. So I lived with this fear that someone would find out I had been in a mental institution, and I kept drinking. The last time I tried suicide was 1957 when I took 100 sleeping pills and drank two-fifths of booze. I woke up in the hospital with wires going in my arm, and my legs, and I started yanking them out. And the doctor asked, "What is wrong with you? Why do you want to die?" I yelled, "I want out of hell."

They said I had no acid in my system, and I had emphysema, (I was dying of that), and pareneshias anemia, and I had to drink liquid acid through a glass tube. I knew that it was time to just get out of this world, so once again, I took an overdose of pills and booze, and once again, I was pronounced dead at the hospital. But I woke up three days later back in Hell.

However, this time I saw my spirit. This experience helped me understand that the spirit within us is separate from the body, and it takes off and goes where it wants to. I saw my spirit running over a beautiful green lawn with a clear blue lake, and I was so happy, crying, "I made it. I finally made it."

This time the doctor gave me two choices. He said, "I can send you back to Patten State Hospital, or you can take up golf."

So I took up golf.

I played golf for two years. To show you the extremist I am, I had to play golf seven days a week. I played barefoot, I played in the rain, the wind, the sun. I had to join seven country clubs. I didn't drink because I played golf every day and was at the driving range every night. My husband and girls had to take up golf also. It was an obsession.

I was made president of the club. Everybody'd get drunk, and there I was, sober. Pollyana, they called me. I took care of them. But I had this LONELY feeling down in the gut. I would go out on the greens and lie there and cry. I didn't know what the loneliness was. Of course, now I know it was the alcoholic me crying to get drunk with them, and yet I knew I couldn't.

One day I missed the tournament by one stroke. I nearly got the big prize. I went into the club and asked the bartender for a drink. He gave me a big glass of vodka. I drank it. And that warm good feeling just came over me. I hadn't drunk for two years, and I thought, Oh, wow! I just took that one drink.

It was January 6, 1960 that I started drinking wine. I began feeling a great unworthiness. I would run away from home and leave notes behind saying things like, "I'm an unworthy mother. I'm an unworthy wife. Go get you another wife." One time I took off on the bus and headed for Arizona. I blacked out, and when I came to again, I was sitting in Blythe, California facing a cop. He was trying to feed me coffee. Next thing I knew, I was in jail. I asked the Captain what happened. He said, "We found you walking up the freeway with a suitcase trying to commit suicide." They called my husband, and he and the girls came to get me.

From then on, I passed over the invisible line of no control. From April until November I totally abandoned myself to alcohol. I drank daily. I no longer hid my bottles. I didn't apologize to my husband. Those nine months are fuzzy in my memory. I just remember drinking and not eating, day in and day out. I started with Canadian Club, and when I couldn't keep that down, I went to wine, and ended up on beer. I was like a zombie.

On the first of November, 1960, I was sitting outside on the patio, watching a walnut tree in front of me as the leaves fell off. It was naked. I looked at the tree and said, "I'm just like you. I'm dead." At that point it didn't make any difference whether I lived or died. I couldn't get sober. I couldn't get drunk. When I drank, I vomited up blood. All I did was just sit and hold this cold beer in my hand. It was Hammns. I loved Hammns. The doctors told me I had three months to live. I was at the point of no return.

The phone rang, and it was my golfing buddy, Opal (she's in Alanon), and she asked me if I'd go and meet some friends. I said, "It doesn't matter." So, she took me to my first AA meeting.

At my first meeting of Alcoholics Anonymous I sat with people who were laughing and giggling, and I heard a man speaking at the podium talking about alcoholics. He said we had an illness. That it was a two-fold disease, an allergy of the body, and an obsession of the mind. And I screamed out, "I'm an alcoholic. I'm not insane. I'm not guilty!"

All these big words that were added after my name made me believe I was insane and everybody else was sane. Nobody went out and lost their car and couldn't find it the next day like I did. Nobody went out and did belly dances while everybody cleared the floor, and somebody'd tell ya what you did the next day. Nobody had the remorse, the guilt, the hate I had for myself as a failure as a mother, a wife, as a human being. There was nobody like me in this world. I was a loner. I was isolated. Into my own little shell.

Now I know alcoholism is a death wish. But it doesn't come in bottles. It comes in people. My body is different from the non-alcoholic. I get one drink in this body, and it sets up a craving, and I gotta satisfy that craving until my cycle is run. I passed over that invisible line where I couldn't control my drinking. I couldn't stop. I lived to drink, and drank to live. No longer did I hide my bottles. No longer did I apologize. I didn't even know I was in this world. It was a great healing to be a zombie. I found out it isn't wrong to hate. I had suppressed my hate. It isn't wrong to make mistakes. It isn't wrong to be a failure.

A failure. What in the hell is a failure? That's man's opinion of what you are doing. I was so afraid of what people would think because that's how I was brought up. If you do that, what will they think. I found out who they are. They are the old ideas I had of myself, of life, and of others.

Then the flood gates opened, and I started crying. I hadn't cried for so long. I say I was baptized by my alcoholic tears. The strange thing was that everyone around me was crying with me. Big Daddy was there (he was six foot 8), and I reached up and said, "You're crying." He looked down at me and answered, "Yes Flo, we love you. We care what happens to you." That's when the candle of hope was lit and my heart opened. I had a stone heart, stone liver, stone everything when I got there. Holes in my pancreas; I had one kidney, and it had cobblestones in it. They took out the gall bladder which had stones in it. I was stoned.

So, you see I didn't ask God to take me, 'cause I didn't know God. This is why I KNOW I have a choice-less awareness! I have no choice. The Grace of God brought me here. It brings all of us here.

At 25 days of sobriety, I went home from a meeting, and I was hurting. I turned on the TV, and there was a Christmas play on. I saw Job on his knees with boils all over, and I thought, that's just the way I feel. Job was saying, "Whether I die, I will trust in Thee." I fell on my boney knees and said, "Whoever you are, whatever you are, teach me. Teach me. Whether I live or die, I'll try to trust in Thee."

Until that time, I'd run out of meetings when they'd say God. I hated Him. I was frightened of Him. And I was one that just couldn't buy the word God or Jesus. But at that time I was willing to try anything.

Then on Thanksgiving my husband was pouring wine at Thanksgiving dinner, and I got the desire to drink. I got in the car and took off to try and find a church, and find some kind of contact with this God. I tried the doors on several churches, but they were all locked. I went up the hill to this Lutheran church, and that door was locked also. I thought, I'll just start the car down the hill. This obsession to drink hit me, and I knew I couldn't drink. I couldn't find God. I couldn't do anything. I was flipping out.

As I started the car over the hill, this hand reached in and turned off the key. The priest said, "Can I help you?"

I told him what was happening to me. He took me in the church and put a little wooden cross in my hand. I looked up and saw a statue of Jesus with His arms and hands outstretched to the side, and it was like I heard Him say, "Come unto me all ye little children, and I will give you rest. My yoke is easy. My burden is light. Learn of me. I am tender and lowly."

The minister told me that was what He was saying, and then he asked me, "Do you believe in Jesus?" I said, "No." "Do you believe in God?" "No!" "Do you believe in the cross?" "NO!" He said, "Well, you belong to AA. They have 12 steps. Now you can take this man as your teacher, and work those 12 steps and find God in your own heart...or you can get in the car and go on down the hill." (I found out later our AA Club was right at the bottom of this church).

I sat there for a long time looking at the statue of Jesus. Suddenly the statue seemed to say, "A merry heart doeth good like medicine." And I started to laugh.

That's when I took Little Boss as my teacher. (A priest gave me that name because I couldn't say Jesus and feel comfortable, but I can say His name now and not rebel against it.) Well, as I say, Jesus touched me and something happened.

I started by asking myself, "What would the Master do?" Like in our Third Tradition when the pure alcoholics were trying to decide who could come to meetings, and one of them said, "What would the Master do?" When I was faced with a decision, I'd ask myself, "What would the Master do?" and when a thought would come to mind to do something, I'd say, "Okay Little Boss," and then I'd do it.

This one morning I woke up at 4 am, and I asked, "Whoever you are, whatever you are, teach me to meditate. Give me a pure heart and an understanding mind." Then I asked, "What do I do now?" The thought came to get a cup of coffee, light a cigarette, and sit there. I did this. After a while, I turned the light on. I wanted to know what words like spiritual and faith meant. I didn't know what faith was, but I know now I was given the gift of blind faith in the beginning, 'cause I didn't have any. So I got the Science of Mind, the Big Book, and the Bible, and I started reading a little bit out of each one. And that's the way I'd start my meditation. When I'd come across something I didn't understand, I'd say, "Now what does that REALLY mean?" Then I'd listen. I didn't know what I was doing. But love-in-action was the magic word. I had hated God so much. (I make amends to God now, 'cause I condemned him for so long for creating all the misery in the world. I found out He didn't do it. That He gave us free will, and we misused it.) Thus, this is the way I started out.

I really didn't know what was happening that first month. I went to meetings, and the steps started working me. I didn't work the steps. I had six sponsors. It took that many to keep me going. One night one of them called me and said, "Are you ready to go to a meeting?" I said, "I can't. I can't move out of the chair." He said, "Bull shit! You just don't want to live." And he hung up the phone.

The hate that came up in me was terrific. Hot and gooey hate. I had always been afraid to say I hated because I thought you weren't supposed to hate. But I was kept alive on hate, because hate, as the reverse of love, is a very strong emotion. Ten minutes later he opened the door and said, "Are you ready to go?"

I'd be sitting there at a meeting crying in my self-pity because the booze was withdrawing, and the body was shaking and filled with pain. (The body was beginning to show how much it had been destroyed.) One of them would say, "Self-pity! Better off dead than the way you are now." Then another one would say, "Hey, you're doing all right."

Then my husband started coming home drunk and told me he didn't love me anymore. I ran to a meeting and asked, "Should I leave him? What shall I do?" One of my sponsors said, "You can't leave him, you gotta take care of the kids and him."

And someone else said, "Well, he's drunk, and if you got drunk, your kids wouldn't have a mother or father. So, I suggest a separation." I decided to leave him.

God goosed me up the steps of AA. Step by Step. My six sponsors kept saying, "Better off dead than the way you are now. Get off your keester and get into action. Go work with somebody." I hated them. How I hated them. How I hated you people. You would sit and laugh, and I would hurt. And I'd say, "You don't know how I hurt." And you'd laugh. And this one guy said, "Just say you're a happy, grateful alcoholic, and act as if you believe it." I said, "How can you be grateful when you're hurtin' so much?" And another guy said, "Well, you know pain is a pleasure." And I said, "Yeah, such a pleasure when it leaves you." They were trying to show me that pain is a healer. 'Cause when you suffer enough, you'll get off your keester and you'll do something about it.

So, as I went along, I became so interested in this love-in-action bit that I forgot about - well, I worked the steps automatically. Making amends? I tried to make amends to my husband that I kicked out to stay sober. He said, "You've said that for 12 years." And I crawled to him on my knees again, and said, "Please forgive me, you gotta forgive me, so I can live." I didn't understand then that as we forgive we are forgiven. I had to forgive him. And I didn't realize how much trouble I caused him until I married an alcoholic in AA, and for 3 1/2 years, he gave me back what I had given out. And I understood the Alanon, what hell they go through. And you know the minute they're gonna pick up a drink by the way they stamp out their cigarette, and that look comes into their eyes.

I took my Fourth Step thirty days after I'd been in AA. I was sitting in a meeting one night, shaking all over, and crying, and this guy said, "Go home. Meditate on your navel and cut the cord on the past."

I wrote my whole life history. My emotional inventory. I walked back through my life, and I reopened every hurt, every wound. It's like divine surgery. And I relived the things that happened to me. I nearly got drunk doing it. I called my sponsor at 2:00 a.m., and I said, "I can't. I want to drink." And he said, "Keep writing or die." I kept writing. I was opening the door to my own book of life. And that's what we are. Life. I'd read many books by many people, but I'd never read my own book.

Sure, people say, "Repent. Seek ye first the kingdom. All these things shall be added." But nobody ever told me HOW to seek the kingdom. As I walked up the ladder of AA, I was shown how: honesty, open-mindedness, willingness. The willingness to hurt. The willingness to give up suffering - my suffering. Happiness is a hard lesson to learn 'cause we feel comfortable miserable. But humility is the healer of all pain.

When I first felt these feelings after my Fourth and Fifth

steps, love-in-action was always my magic words. When I'd be overcome by these body changes as I'd call them, I'd step out and work with the sick alcoholic. I volunteered my services at the hospital and began working with broken bodies. I decided my body wasn't as bad off as their bodies.

AA teaches us that as we align our will with His great will, it's His pleasure to give us the kingdom. And the kingdom for us alcoholics is the living flame of AA. It's the living flame of love. 'Cause it's people just like you that picked up this devastated body that could not live, and healed me through your love, through your patience, through your laughter.

I hadn't laughed for so long, and when I learned to laugh at me, it was so strange. They kept telling me, "Talk or you're gonna die." So one night I thought, Okay I'll tell them the experience in Reno when I was beat up and left on the bar room floor to die. When I told them, they all laughed. You don't know how that hurt. This self-centeredness I had when I came into this program. I thought, nobody knows how I hurt.

It was confusing at first. I'd read the Big Book, and it says we are selfish and self-centered in the extreme, that we've got to get rid of this selfishness or it kills us. Then I'd hear some guy say, "This is a selfish program." It used to blow my mind.

So I began studying. My sponsor would call me for a meeting, and I'd say, "I'm sorry but I'm going to bed with Matthew tonight." And he'd say, "Who in the hell is Matthew?" I'd say, "You know, the guy in the Bible." And he'd say, "Oh my God, she's studying the Bible, and will probably become a fanatic."

But all of a sudden I got this one-pointed viewpoint - that every human being was a potential alcoholic. As I studied the Bible, I saw these guys as alcoholics, and their words simply the way they understood God. I see now that by His grace and by trying to relate everything I studied to our Twelve Steps and Twelve Traditions, it kept me emotionally balanced.

I became Executive Director of Mental Health, and started working with mentally retarded children, and working with the sick so-called mental patients and alcoholics. Working the principles of AA. Putting Little Boss's words into living action. We opened the doors of Patten State Hospital, and I can see how my experience in Patten as a patient helped me work with them on the outside.

We used to give parties for them, and bring them to the Half-Way house, as we called it, and the psychiatrist would come around and ask, "How do you do it?" I'd say, "Through love and understanding." "But it's not possible," he'd answer. And I'd say, "Through love, it is. It's happening." They couldn't believe.

Every time I tried to understand it, Little Boss would say, "What's that to you? I said to follow me. Love-in-action are the magic words. Go LOVE somebody today without a price tag. Smile at somebody. Sing a song. Do something for somebody today."

I'd go to meetings, and I'd get these strange feelings within me, and I'd tell them how I'd feel, and they'd say, "That's self pity." And I'd say, "No, it's something else." So that's when I turned to my books, and the Saints. St. John of the Cross, St. Theresa, St. Francis of Assisi. I try to live his prayer daily. Better to love than be loved. I never knew how to love, and didn't know what it was all about.

All of a sudden, St. John of the Cross was explaining what was happening to me. I was experiencing "the dark night of the soul." The soul, my soul was waking up. And it wasn't easy. I'd feel like I was a nothing. It was like stepping out into an abyss, and not feeling. But I used to say to my body, "Do the thing you fear to do, and it'll turn into faith. Make it hard on yourself. Easy on others."

So many times my body couldn't get out of bed. The spirit would take off and say, "You're supposed to be dead anyway," so...pretty soon, here comes the body.

Then I found Tom Merton, and his Seeds of Contemplation. He began helping me, and all of a sudden the light of understanding would come. I saw the Twelve Steps as the Eight Beatitudes, the Eight-Fold path of Buddha, the Koran of Mohammed. AA is and has a combination of all these put together telling us how to accept our humanity. I didn't want to be human. It hurt too much. AA teaches us to accept our humanity - firmly but gently. From out of the depths of hell, it takes us to the heights of heaven and allows us a spiritual awakening.

It was a year and a half after I'd been in AA that I came home from work, and the pains had taken over my body. I started getting liver attacks. I called the head of the Board and said, "I have to quit. " She said, "You can't."

But Love-in-action are the magic words. I went to the Bible as I usually did, closed my eyes and put my finger down on a page I'd opened to. It said, "If you can't leave houses, husbands, children, wives and follow me, you're not worthy of me." And Cherie was there, she was 14 at the time, I think, and I said, "You want to come with me? I've got to leave. I have to leave everything." Then I turned to the Big Book and it said, "We're willing to go to any length for victory over alcohol."

I called Walt and asked him if he wanted to get back together, and he said he'd never had it so good. I told him he could have the house, get a divorce. He could have everything. I didn't want anything. We had $30,000 worth of liquid assets. This is the hardest thing I've had to do in AA, let go of all these things.

We ended up in Imperial Beach in the sand dunes. My car stopped. It wouldn't run any further. So I took my gear and went out on the sand dunes, and I stayed there for 40 days. Cherie went to San Diego with a friend, and I was alone with my pain.

I was on a little island, and there were hundreds of seagulls and pelicans there. In the morning they'd rise up and fly. The pelicans were so beautiful, and I'd feel lifted up. Several times in my mind I'd think I'd already died and gone to heaven with the birds.

The pains in my body were getting so horrible, my ankles were swelling, and one morning I just lay down, and said, "OK, I'm ready." I knew I was dying. And the obsession to drink hit me. I looked at the ocean and thought it was vodka. I crawled down to get a drink, and crawled back up. I don't know how long this went on. But as I was lying there, suddenly there was a stillness. I mentally saw the universe as pure light vibrating. I spiritually experienced it. All knowledge was open to me. I saw that everything was light, everything was perfect in its changing form. Only thing is people don't know it. They have to wake up.

And the vibrations...like 10,000 volts of electricity went through my body. I call it the Virgin Birth of the Christ, Christ consciousness. Every birth of the Christ is a virgin birth...God gives it to us.

And I started laughing. I started laughing because I saw the divine comedy. I had been trying so hard, and I hadn't been doing anything. It was God Himself doing it all. Then I got angry and said, "Up Your bucket. Up Your Divine bucket!" Suddenly the seagulls took off, and it was so beautiful. That was July of 1962. I've never been the same since.

I was given the gift of Divine love. My body started healing. It was about two weeks later that the cops found me. I had made three rooms out there. And the cops had never seen them because the dunes were pretty high. I was black because there were no trees, and I had liver spots all over me. Sometimes I had to dig holes in the sand and put the towel up to keep out of the sun. I really didn't know how weird I looked.

So, one morning I was standing next to the refrigerator that the ocean had brought me, buttering a little piece of bread when I saw these boots. I looked up at the cop, and he looked at me and said, "You can't live here. You'll go to jail if you're not out of here by morning." I had been there 40 days, and Cherie had returned to join me. I said, "Oh, Okay."

After he left I started crying because I was married to the ocean, and I didn't want to leave it. And I knew I wouldn't be back.

We returned to Riverside, and I went to a meeting with all my sponsors, and I said "My God! We're all one big glob of God!" And they said, "Oh, you been drunk?" I said, "Yup, drunk on spiritual wine. We're all one big glob of God."

The words that started coming out of my mouth, like love, and God is love, and we're all expressions of love, and all we gotta do is just love each other - were far out; I was floating.

The Divine Gift of Love was given to me, and it flowed out of me so much that people ran from me 'cause I just loved 'em so much. Because all of a sudden it was the love, you know, the love you can't see. And I went through this thing of going to the bars saying, "Hey, you don't have to suffer anymore. Come on with me". That's when they started calling me Flobird. 'Cause I'd talk about the seagulls and the pelicans, and that's when I became a seagull. And that's when I completely abandoned my life to humanity, when I fell in love with God, when I fell in love with you. And that's what my life is dedicated to today. I was asked to speak at jails, churches. They said, "You've got the Holy Ghost" and I'd say, "I must. It ain't me."

I was talking in the jail one night, and there were about 80 birds there, and I was brand new from my spiritual awakening. I was talking about "be like the birds in the air, they neither sow nor reap nor gather in the barn, 'cause they KNOW their heavenly Father feeds them." All these things were popping out of me, and after my pitch the jail psychiatrist come up to me and said, "Do you REALLY think you're a seagull?" He had that look in his eye.

They were such joyous times. Pure joy. People would look at me and run, and I'd bless 'em, and it didn't bother me inside, until all of a sudden, I walked in the Alano club one day, and one of the guys said, "Let go and let Flo." And I thought, that isn't right, it's Let Go and Let God. I looked at him, and said, "Have I been playing God?" He said, "Well honey, you've been grabbing 'em off the bar stool, and telling them they don't have to suffer anymore. This isn't the way it works."

And I went home and started crying, 'cause I got this understanding that I couldn't take anyone's suffering away from them. I could only walk with them, and share my suffering. And that's when I started going through the dark night of the soul again.

I had this idea that if you had a spiritual awakening, you wouldn't hurt no more. But that's when the hurting starts. The hurt for other people. When you love 'em so much, and they come at you with this cold hate, and you can't make them see, that's when you start hurting. And this is when you start learning what Jesus went through.

When I was in Israel, we had a little cave there by the Red Sea. I saw Him walking, talking, healing, loving, and no one could understand. No one could accept that He's still there doing the same thing. But in Israel, it seemed like something happened to me that has never left me either. It was this feeling of, "it's all right." "Everyone will make it." "No one will be lost." It's just a point of time of understanding, and the Christ is our own heart, and we are the Christ of God, the love of God - the love that won't stop flowing, the love that heals us instantly in AA.

You don't recognize it, but we're instantly healed. We don't drink any more. We don't have to be out there dying anymore. All we have to do is work the 12 Steps. Follow directions. Go within our own being and find out who we are. We are life. We are love. We are joy. We're gonna live forever somewhere. This is the message of AA.

Well, I went to Hawaii and married an alcoholic. He was a man of knowledge. He kept getting drunk every seven months. And it was fascinating. I watched him go from a gentleman who was a principal of high schools with all these degrees to the monster stage which is the last stage of alcoholism. He tried to ram me with an ironing board. My youngest daughter, Marchand, was with us at the time, and she grabbed the board away from him as I ran from the house. She tried to shield me from him by standing between us. I finally had to leave him. That was 1967.

So I began my career following my heart. And everybody would say, "That's impossible, you can't do it." And I'd say, "With God all things are possible." I found I can keep my head in the clouds, but my feets have to be on the ground.

I stood in the universe with no visible means of support. I slept on the beach. I hung this body in a tree. It was Love-in-action. I started living in the tents with the hippies in Hawaii -- 1967-68. Many of them would walk into the open meetings, and be high on acid, and they'd say, "I'm God." I'd say, "Well, hi God. Sit down. Let's talk. Now, if you think you're God, go hold the ocean back with your hands, and tell me, do you know how to love? Can you love?" "Well, no." "Well, God is love, so how can you be God if you're not loving."

They're sooo beautiful. I love 'em. And I understand these young ones that are on acid and pot and all these drugs. And I've worked with some that people thought were totally hopeless like me. And they're back in the world again, doing their thing, off drugs. They'd stay with me until they took the Fourth and Fifth Steps, and they'd take off and make their amends.

I found out these so called hippies are the intellects. They didn't want to hurt. This acid put them way up there on a high, and I'd sit with them in their lotus, and they'd pass the pipe around, and I'd say, "No thanks, I'm on a permanent high." "How'd you get that way?" "Oh, read the Big Book and work the steps, and you'll find out." And some of them got the message. I have little birds like this all over the world.

And this is when I started saying, "I'm an alcoholic-drug addict", 'cause I saw the speed, and all these things they were taking - see, I took it too, only I called it Dexedrine, Phenobarbital, Demerol, it's the same thing, different names.

We started our Beachcombers Spiritual Progress Traveling Group in March of 1968, and we began saying "I'm an alcoholic-drug addict." Alcohol's another drug. Many people don't think so. We had many adventures, lived in tents on the Big Island of Hawaii, and by faith we got fed. We ate many things. Breadfruit, herbs - and we never went hungry. We had to go through these things to prove by faith that God was God and all things were possible.

I woke up one morning near the end of 1970, and in my meditation I got, "Go to Egypt by boat." told the group that was with me, "I gotta go to Egypt. Anybody want to go with me?" I had four volunteers, and we went to Egypt by boat. But it took us 10 months, and that was 10 months by faith, and it was fantastic, the things that happened to us, the way we were fed.

God sent me to Europe first. I had a bird in the army that was climbing the walls 'cause he was the only sober one there. Everybody smoked pot and shot up heroin around him. So, Love-in-action are the magic words, and off to Germany we went. They only had one meeting there when we arrived, and when we left they had seven meetings a week. The army was asking us to start a meeting in every barracks, and we had to tell the General that AA was attraction and not promotion. Working with the army boys was pretty rough because they were into heroin and the harder stuff. Seven of 'em OD'd one night.

They'd come to me, and they'd been shootin' up in the arm, and they'd sit, and I'd look at 'em and then say, "Have you ever tried morphine?" And they'd say, "No." I'd say, "Go try it." You know, get it out of your system. If you haven't tried shootin' up in your hands, use your hands, or use your toes. Get it out of your system. Hit bottom - if you still want to die. If you want to live, I'll go to any length to help you." You see, AA teaches us to uncover and discover our real selves. Know the truth, and it will set us free.

In Germany the priest asked me to speak at the church. And when he got to the little thing about, "Be like the birds in the air. They neither sow, nor reap nor gather in barns because they know their heavenly father feeds them," he called on me to talk and asked me if any of my family was there. I said, "Any alcoholic, or drug addict in church today, will you please stand." And quite a few stood. I said, "This is my family all over the world. Every alcoholic and drug addict in the universe is my family." And then I started my little ol' pitch, and there were a lot of so called colored people there, and I looked at one of them, and he was crying. And I said, "What color is God's skin?" This would be a hell of a universe if everything was the same color. You know, we're like little flowers.

Then I apologized. I said, "You guys were going to church. At least you had a direction, while I was lying in my vomit and crawling and condemning all you good people. So please forgive me." And I turned to the priest and I said, "Please forgive me." I'll never forget it. The wonderful, beautiful feeling I had. And when the priest grabbed me and kissed me, that was something else, because what would the Pope think.

We bought a van and took off for Egypt via France and Spain. The bird that was in the army, finished his tour of duty and came with us. In France I broke a rib, so we had to stop in Rota, Spain where it could mend. We didn't have any money as usual, but went to a meeting. An Alanon was sitting there, Casey, I believe was her name. She said, "My house is yours." She took us all into her house right on the beach where the seagulls flew, and there my rib mended through Love-in-action. The girls went to work as bartenders, and made enough money for us to travel on, but while there, we met a couple that are here tonight. I haven't seen them since we were in Spain, and that's Betty and Rick. Via the grapevine they heard that we were here, and came over to see us last night. This is what happens in AA. You never know when you're going to meet some of your birds.

From Spain we took off over Northern Morocco, the Atlas mountains. There was just a little trail, and the navy boys told us, "You know, it's primitive. The Arabs will jump out at you." And we said, "Fine. Love-in-action are the magic words." They did jump out at us. I'd give 'em my passport, and they'd hold it upside down, and look at us and grin. And we'd silently bless them and pretty soon, they'd laugh and give 'em back. All of a sudden I knew they were using vibrations. They could pick up the vibration of fear, and we were so mindless, we had nothing to fear.

Anyway, we hit Benghazi, Libya in December of 1971, out of money again, so we sold our clothes. They loved the clothes we had. We were sitting by the ocean this one afternoon, and didn't know what we were going to do next. The next boat didn't go out until the 26th, and we didn't have any money. We were all hungry. Suddenly these beautifully dressed Arabs walked up to the van (Ladybird we called her), opened the door, handed us two huge sandwiches, and said, "Could we help you?"

They gave us a little apartment to live in, and lo and behold, Cherie, Marchand and I and the baby got on the boat and went to Egypt. We had one American dollar, and 10 Egyptian piesties

I didn't know what Egypt would be like. I didn't know that white slavery still existed. I didn't know many things - all I knew was Love-in-action were the magic words. God provides where He guides. We were kicked out in the main street of Cairo with many events happening around us. So I took a sweater I was wearing and tried to sell it. They laughed at me. A cop looked at us, and a voice hollered out, "May I help you?" It was a Lebanese University student. He took us home.

We carried our message of live, love, laugh and be happy. That's God's will for us. "Who are you?" They'd ask. "We're alcoholics!" They'd never heard of AA; they'd never heard of Little Boss. We stayed there 18 days. When they'd leave the apartment, they would lock the doors. We were made prisoners, and that is when our faith set in. They were trying to make the girls go to bed with them. One night they were all like wolves, and I told them they were like a bunch of wolves in sheep's clothing, and all these things come out of my mouth, and they just stood there and looked at me. They were scared. This two edge sword of love that can come out of our hearts, works, it really does.

In Lebanon a priest had to help us. We were sleeping on a hill 'cause we didn't have any money again. And I was sitting there meditating, and all of a sudden I heard goats. These huge goats were surrounding me, and I said, "Okay Little Boss, what'll I do now? If I move, they'll jump on me." Then I heard this little giggle. There stood this little Arab with no teeth. I gave him a cigarette, and he called his goats off.

Anyway, it started raining. We were headed for the street and this big black car come by and it was nearly dark, and it happened to be a priest. "What are you doing out here with a baby (2 year old)?!" I said, "Well, we're following Little Boss." He said, "Who's Little Boss?" I said, "Well, it's Jesus. We're trying to do what He wants us to do." And he says, "Jesus was a carpenter, and he was a practical man. He did not go sleeping on mountains." Well, I couldn't tell him that he did. So he took us to this school that he had for deaf and dumb children, and he called all over Lebanon trying to find a place for us to stay. And he called his nuns, and they had a boarding house, and one of the birds was sitting in the office, and they heard the nun say, "But hippies? We don't give places to hippies." And David said the priest said, "I was hungry, and you fed me. I was naked, and you clothed me." And he slammed down the phone. And I sat there and thought, you know - he's trying to put off on somebody else what God gave him to do. It's just like the alcoholic when somebody calls us for a 12 step call, and we say well, we gotta watch color TV or call so and so.

So finally the Priest gave us 25 pounds a piece, and called a cab in order to salvage his own conscience. He couldn't stand us. Anyway, he put us in a cab, and I reached over to kiss him, a gratitude kiss, and he said, "Don't touch me. What would the Pope think!" And we just started giggling.

As I look back on these things, it was all on faith, 'cause we didn't know where we were going. All we knew was that it was one day at a time.

From Lebanon we went to Cypress, but they wouldn't let us in Cypress 'cause we didn't have any money. As usual. They were going to send us back to Lebanon, and I said, "Well, we can't go to work in Lebanon." So the American Ambassador came. "Where do you want to go?" he asked. I told him, "If we could get to Israel, we could go to work and pay for our passage."

A pilot was standing there; they were holding the plane we wanted to take. I started talking about God. They asked me what I was doing, and I said, "Well, we're a group in AA." He said, "Do you think God would fly that plane?" And I said, "Well, of course. Who else?" We got into a discussion about what God could do and what He couldn't do. And pretty soon we had all the officials around us. The American Ambassador looks at 'em, and all of a sudden I knew he Okayed the whole thing. So I walked up, and I kissed him on the cheek, and he said, "It's OK." I nearly asked him if he was in AA.

But somehow we got to Israel with $10, I think. And as we landed I felt this feeling I've felt in Hawaii - I'm home. I'm home. I never wanted to leave there. We went out to the Elat desert, and found a rock house without a roof. We called it our rock cave.

I can understand the Psalms now because we went through the life they describe. And we went to Galilee. The picture I've had in my mind's eye of Jesus was a red-headed, blue-eyed, very tall man - a joy boy. When we went to Nazareth and Galilee, I discovered the Galileans are red-headed and blue-eyed. It was if I had been there when He walked the land. It's not very holy now. In fact, it's very unholy.

It was in Israel that I discovered where the Holy Ground was. I discovered that Christ is still walking this earth - talking, healing, loving each one of us in our own hearts.

We were called American Bedouins 'cause we didn't have any place to live except this cave that we found, and the other Bedouins with their camels, slept under a tree, and they took care of us. They carried guns. And we'd talk with our eyes. They'd come over and look at me, and I'd give em a cigarette, and they'd go, "uh huh," and they'd go away.

As I lay in bed one night, these words came to me, "On this rock I will build my church and all the gates of hell cannot prevail against it." I thought, oh, the rock is our heart. And all the thoughts of hell, all these old ideas can't prevail against it. The Christ child is born in our own heart, and we feed it until it grows and grows and we give birth to Christ consciousness. Christ consciousness is realizing that we are the light, we are the way, the truth and the light. Everyone is. Everyone is chosen. God created us for companionship. But we didn't understand 'cause nobody ever told us how to love, to live, 'till we came to AA.

We stood at the sea of Galilee, and as I was looking out over the sea, I saw a big rainbow. I punched Doug and said, "Look at this rainbow!" An Arab man came up and grabbed my cross and said, "Are you a Christian?" I said, "No, I'm an alcoholic." When I was given this cross in 1961, Mama Barelli said, "I shouldn't give it to you, you're not a Catholic." I said, "Well, neither was Jesus." She still hasn't forgiven that one.

I didn't know Jesus' last name wasn't Christ. Jesus became the Christ. I was so igernant, you know. But today I know who Jesus is, I know who I am, I know who you are. I know where we're going. What we're here for. It took me 42 years. I died many times. To learn, to grow in understanding of God, of ourselves, and it's all through the teachings of AA. God is love, and works through our heart. And that's AA - a living flame of love. Brings 'em back alive.

I'll have to tell you about Connie. I think some of you know her. The last time she came in, she said she wanted to jump in the ocean and die. I said, "Try it. I did and I got thrown out on the beach." She said, "I don't want to live in this world anymore. The evil spirits are eating me up." I worked with her for a week and a half. They found her body washed ashore. She left her books behind. My name is in it, and all the birds here. And she had a picture of Cherie and Tom. They are still looking for a guy that was with her. They aren't sure whether it was suicide or whatever. The cops come across the words Little Boss in her book, and said, "Who is Little Boss?" I looked at him and said, "Well, that's what we call Jesus." He said, "Oh." I tried to explain to him, and all of a sudden he said, "Can I come on your side? We bring 'em back dead, and you bring 'em back alive."

So that's kinda what it's all about. AA has come of age now. There are so many things that I want to say...the best is yet to come. The best is yet to come. Mass awakenings are happening. Everyone is knowing. There is no inferior, no superior. All equal. Individual, unique, expressing our own spiritual talent, and we're all here to love, and serve, and tell you that God loves you.

And AA is our protective mantel from all these other teachings. I had to study all the yoga paths, Hinduism, Mohammedism, Yogananda, and all these other paths. I studied, I practiced the principles, and they all come down to love and service. Love each other. It's all within our own hearts. To uncover and discover my real self. We don't have to sit and say, "OM" all day long to contact God as some of the birds did when I first met them. They'd be sooo serious sittin' in their Lotus.

God wants us to live, love, laugh and be happy. JOY is our true nature! That's why we yearn to be happy, yearn to quit hurting, 'cause our true nature is JOY. Our purpose is to love each other. It's so simple and yet so hard to do because all these old ideas are like a broken record right down here in the gut. We have to get 'em out through the Fourth and Fifth steps, and throw the rest away to keep on uncovering and discovering. I've been asked, "How do you know God talks to you?" "Well, how do you know a bird sings? You listen." We're all channels of God's love. Unique. He never repeats Himself. So let's love each other.

Life is a spiritual school. As we learn one lesson, another lesson comes up. It's never ending. Like the new teaching coming out of the universe now. The science of triangles of energy, of light, of auras, reincarnation (if you don't believe it, look again, it's true). I have relived several of my past lives. God, I had a horrible Karma. But, we just need to live each day, one day at a time, have an open mind and open heart and open hands.

We are the Cross. These are our Traditions. These are our Steps. The cross of AA - and right here is the love that keeps flowing out to everyone. Not only AA, but all humanity. You see, those that aren't alcoholics, they don't have that devastating obsession that we have, and have to find another way of life. Overeating, sex, something like that. If we drink again, we die. I don't have another drunk left. I know if I took one drink, I'd get out of this body, and I'm not gonna go unless I take it with me. I tried to lose it for 42 years. Now I want to stay for all the fireworks.

The next 20 years are going to be wonderful. And all we gotta do one day at a time is to love each other and help the next drunk, the next human being that comes into our life. God means for us to have an abundance, inner and outer. It's His pleasure to give us the kingdom.

You see, I never thought God wanted me to have pleasure. I thought I had to give up bowling, tennis, dancing, cards. The SERIOUSNESS of it in the beginning. Everything I did was supposedly a sin. I hated the word sin, I hated religion. Now I know that sin is missing the mark, and we learn the lesson through our suffering. When we become willing to give up our suffering, we take the second step - humility. God is the doer. We are the channel. The little will gets in there and says, I want more. Our greatest glory is that we don't have to drink today. We don't have the obsession to die, to go into oblivion.

The greatest joy is watching the lights come on in people's eyes. Watching the sick drug addicts that are soo dead, come alive. And to listen to people laughing. It isn't pain, it's laughter from the belly. To watch the joy of living emerge out of Alcoholics Anonymous. It's a paradox.

I used to think, love your enemies. I loved alcohol. But at first it was my friend, then it became my enemy. And now it's my friend again because it keeps me on this path.

And our Twelve Steps go within us, and reveal to us our TRUE, REAL, self. The self that is not afraid of anything or anybody, 'cause fear of people, places, and things in our own mind is what's been keeping us chained, chained to death. We have been dead. And now we're awakening. There is a spiritual awakening all over the world.

God Himself is preparing all of us for the things that are coming into this world. Into this earth now. The United States is hitting bottom just like we did. The false security of our nation right now is hitting bottom.

And the things that are going to happen within the next ten years...you must maintain peace, love, and joy. Start loving each other as we are all God's own self. The revelations in the Bible are happening right now. The earthquakes, the tidal waves, the cosmic solar events are coming to our planet. This is why we've got to wake up. To wake up and help others.

Alcoholism, drug addiction, all these things, are only a symbol of our deeper sickness, our spiritual soul sickness. Wanting to be free. To be free to be me. And to know that you're free. You see. This is what it's all about.

So join us. Let's uncover and discover - God is right here within. God in us, as us, is us. Let us accept it! Let's quit crawling. Let's accept our divine nature. Jesus was an able example. What I have done, you can do. He showed us how. AA shows us how to wake up. This brings a spiritual awakening - we awaken to our true nature. We are spirits in a little garment, and love is our true nature.

Jesus is a joyous man. He says, "So my joy may be fulfilled." And if you count the joys, the love and the peace in the new testament, you'll see that's all it talks about. The simple teachings, to love God is to love each other without judgment. And to recognize when you meet somebody else, that they're a human being too. And they have the same emotions, the same hurts, the same problems that we all have. So who are we to condemn anybody. No longer do I separate myself from humanity. I am one with all humanity. And I hurt all humanity by trying to kill myself through ignorance at first.

But I'm not igernant any longer. I have divine bliss now. Divine igernance is bliss. I don't know what I'm going to do until I do it. I follow my heart, and when it says prepare to leave this place I prepare, and I wait. Go here, go there. And the green energy is there.

I work 24 hours a day. Spiritual work is 24 hours a day. My work is love and service. My old idea of work was get the money baby. No more. It's where can I give the most love and service. God is my employer, and He doesn't pay my wages much in green energy. He pays my wages in sick little birds that come with broken wings. And through the AA program, I help them mend those wings.

God is our sponsor. He's our teacher. Many people have tried to make me their teacher, and I don't want that burden. What I have learned, we all know in our hearts. We all have these talents. We don't have to crawl anymore. We can stand on our own two feet and walk tall. 'Cause God has forgiven us, so how about us forgiving ourselves. 'Cause it's in forgiveness that we are forgiven. It is in loving that we are loved. And as we walk along God will reveal more to you and to me. And we can't transmit something we haven't got. We can only try to put it into loving action.

There is so much to learn. I continue to study. I continue to work. I continue to meditate. It seems like lately all I've been doing is watching and praying. Then I get this divine restlessness - let me go do something. But not yet. There's a period of time in which we have to learn patience. Patient endurance obtainith all things. I have many teachers. St. Francis, St. Theresa, all the saints. They were sinners that kept on trying. Just like us.

No longer do I defy God. I don't need to. I have no power.

Humility is knowing you're powerless over life, death and all that's in it and being happy about it. I can only continue sharing my experience, strength and hope with everyone that enters my life. Our door has never been locked. People walk in and out any time of the day.

We had a battle on the Big Island of Hawaii back in the '70's when the hippies and the so-called Primo Warriors were fighting. Every morning we'd wake up - a hippie would be dead, beaten up. The long hair, beard. The Primo Warriors were a group of Hawaiians that hated the whites. They were all alcoholics. So I invited them all in. They became my friends. Most of them now are in AA or in NA. So we become fearless. Love never gives up. I stick with the losers.

There's only one law in this universe, and that's love. Everything in the universe gives. We didn't know how to give. We didn't know how to love. These 12 Steps show us. So let's open our book of life. Let's start LOVING each other as God loves us without a price tag. He means for us to have an abundance out here as well as in here. So let's go. Let's help God balance this universe.

As it says in our A Vision For You, abandon yourselves to God as you understand God. Do away with the wreckage of your past. Give freely of that which you find. Admit your faults to God, yourself, and your fellow man, and I'm sure we'll meet some of you in the fellowship of the spirit as we trudge this road to our happy destiny. God bless us and keep us everyone. Thank you.

2

FLOBIRD'S EYE VIEW

Gratitude is reverence for life. I didn't have any for 42 years.
-- Flobird

Flobird sent letters via cassette tapes filled with inspiring and thought-provoking experiences covering various subjects as well as sharing her pain, sorrow and happiness. She could start talking about one particular subject and end up talking about something completely different. What follows is a compilation of those tape-letters beginning with her sharing on certain topics and ending with her experiences while in the depth of her physical pain from cancer.

GOD

My name is Flobird, and I am a happy, grateful alcoholic and drug addict, living today only by the Grace of God in AA, and THAT is rigorous honesty. Well, God is a name that man has given to the great thing called life, life abundant. God to me is love, peace, joy, happiness, all these attributes, but you really can't name God. You can't really describe God. 'Cause He's the one who can not be named. God is energy. Energy is light in motion cascading into many rainbows. We're all little rainbows set in the big rainbow.

So to me, God is all there really is expressing Himself in His many life forms. And love without a price tag is His greatest gift to all of us. It's very simple. All we have to do is live, love, laugh, be blissed out, joyous, be happy. Happiness is wanting what we get. Unhappiness is getting what we think we want. Blissed out is an empty think tank and just living by the spirit. You don't know what you're gonna do until you do it. You look back and see how beautiful it was.

Beauty is another attribute of God. Everywhere you look, there's beauty. Birds are very spiritual beings. Look up and watch them fly, and watch the beautiful aerial joy they have when the wind's blowing. They rejoice in life. The human being doesn't know how to rejoice in living. He's always too busy getting. God is the greatest servant of us all. He's always giving to all of us. And we have to go within ourselves and clean out all the old ideas of who, what, and where God is.

God is our very own self. Spirit and body is one. We've always misused the body thinking it was evil and corruptible.

Now we are finding out it's the living soul. And the body is the Christ of God in form. Christ means light or love. When you become acquainted with your own body temple and find it IS God in form, you change your attitude towards it, and try to take care of it, really take care of it by telling it it IS beautiful and wonderfully made. Then God starts molding us in His image as we get rid of all our false images of ourselves.

God is one. We are one. We are all an expression of God. We are all an expression of life, and of love. And the transition on the planet right now is the Kingdom of Heaven right here on earth, and we seem to have one foot in heaven and one foot on earth. The transition is that everybody doesn't know what to do now. They want to express their spiritual talents which are human talents, and that's the divine comedy. 'Cause spirit is human in form. And the very simplicity and the very practical way of living is to be here now. Live in the now and accept our abundance of life. And every human being we meet, to see that he, too, is an expression of life, of love, of God, if you wanna call it God.

God is very simple. It's like waking up in the morning and rejoicing in another day. Making all things new. Listening to the song of the bird, listening to the wind and ocean roar. This is all God expressing Himself in everything.

It seems to take what it takes to accept that God wants us to live, love, laugh and be happy. To accept our abundance. It's fantastic! His amazing Grace. If we keep on keepin' on, and keep trying to talk to Him just like I'm talking to you, He starts answering back - if we'll listen. It's like the mind - it's going all the time. It doesn't have time to listen. God is our every heartbeat, our every breath - without our breath we couldn't live. Our breath is the Holy Ghost. Every word we speak becomes God in manifest. It's very simple. God bless you all.

***

AA is a spiritual underground. In other words, it's no religion. It's a protective mantel. You know, they come up and ask, "Are you a Christian?" and I say, "No, I'm an alcoholic." So it's God as I understand Him. And this is what our community will be based on, a universal church of God as love expressing Himself as life - in unity.

God does love us and is trying to tell us that He does want to provide for us. All we have to do is hold out our hands and accept all His beautiful treasures which come from our Father in Heaven. So, be of good cheer.

***

Sometimes it's very difficult to keep giving love when so much hate keeps coming back at you, but I have to keep remembering what I used to be like when I first came to AA, so full of hate because I really wanted to die and couldn't. And people like you appeared from out of the bushes, and set my feet right upon this crooked path. God makes our crooked path straight. All we have to do is keep on asking Him to teach us to keep giving love for hate. That's the answer. Love without a price tag.

Little did I know what was on this path when God brought me to AA. He chose me, I didn't choose Him. And He just keeps me keepin' on. So many people here, in some of the little towns think I'm absolutely insane, a witch, and all these things that we are called when man doesn't understand us. It's like contempt before investigation. But we just keep on keepin' on. Inch by inch it's a cinch, and we just keep doing good to those who hurt us, and bless those who persecute us, loving our enemies within ourselves and without.

The last enemy to overcome is fear of death which is really fear of God, and hell, and fire, and damnation. And all we alcoholics and drug addicts have been in every department of Hell, and now we're in our Heaven right here on earth. Heaven is a state of peace, love, and joy no matter what the condition is. Divine love is the answer. God DOES have a plan for us. And the best is yet to come. His divine plan is for all humanity to awaken to their oneness - God in expression. The Christ is us. The Christ means love. So, just keep trying to communicate with God, He's in your little ol' heart. Dare to follow your heart.

***

You know, it's a strange thing, our minds have to be entertained. That's why we have to let go, and let the Spirit take over our minds, and we become that which we think about. If you constantly think about God, and living, loving, laughing and being happy, that's what you become. God is very personal, or impersonal. You can look out of your eyes at abundant life, or you can stay locked in your little self-centered house. But the more you expand your awareness, the more you let go and let God lead your life, the more you become a living example of what AA teaches us - to be free. To be free of all people's opinion, and our own opinion of ourselves.

As Doctor Schuller said today, we put ourselves down. And since we can put ourselves down, we can surely raise ourselves up with the help of God. God wants us to be happy. He wants us to have an abundance, and money is fine. But it's the right use and right dependence on it. We have a golden abundance daily if we live in the now.

***

God is life energy changing form. When I tell people my Higher Power is the sun, 'cause without the sun we couldn't live, they think I'm a kook, but that's OK. God is light, love, peace and joy. And these are all the qualities of God. Energy is all there really is here. We live and move and breathe and have our being in energy. Energy in motion. We are constantly moving, changing form.

And there really isn't any authority here except our own understanding of life. 'Cause God is life, and we are the way, the truth, and the life. Once we get rid of all our old ideas (you know, our human mind is so conditioned to believe what other people say,) when we really transmute all those old ideas and have an empty think tank, then we're in touch with the unknown.

***

I don't care what you call God. God is only a name that man has given to something he doesn't understand. I call it life, light, love. Call It anything you want. God must be an alcoholic 'cause He's so anonymous. You know, it's people like you that show me where God is. What He is. It's people like you that listened to my woes, my poor little me's. It took a lot of humiliation for me to find humility. To humble myself before you and say, "I am a failure." I can't even quit smoking.

But then along comes those joy periods. Those glimpses that God gives us of the vision for ourselves. We are God's people. We're nobody else's. I didn't choose God. He chose me. I didn't choose AA. It chose me. I was at the end of the road. And I still come to the ends of these roads. And I say, "OK God, is this all there really is? Let's get on with the show. Do I have to sit here and listen to all these Fourth and Fifth Steps day in and day out? Can't we talk about joy and love and peace?" And that's gettin' spiritual pride.

When you have a vision, you see that the best is yet to come, that we were all born to wake up to our real being, our spiritual being, we're all expressions of love. In God's eyes, we're all equal.

It's only in our own old ideas that we're not equal. And AA allows us to be stupid. AA allows us to change our minds 50 dozen times a day. AA doesn't demand you believe in anything. I didn't believe in anything when I got here. I didn't even know what faith was. I didn't know what being spiritual meant. Or what meditation was.

***

In the beginning God made us in His image and likeness. And we got selfish and decided to make our own images. And kinda messed up the image, right? So now these are the old images you have to get rid of 'cause God just will not be made in our image and likeness. We have to uncover and rediscover the real image of light and love and beauty, eternal life.

You know, God is very emotional. He expresses Himself in the negative, positive, and any ol' way if you just swing with it. We are transmuting the ancient feelings of guilt through our false ideas of who we are. This golden temple of God, you know, this Kingdom which is our body has many rooms, and we can clean out each little room one day at a time to find many jewels in each room. It's just a give-a-way program

And instead of talking so much to God, just sit and listen, and He'll tell you what it's all about. He doesn't have many listeners on this planet. There's too many that get a little knowledge and run with it. But knowledge by itself never kept us sober. It has to be taken into the heart and turned into the wisdom to know the difference. And as you read your Bible you can read it on four levels. Mental, emotional, physical or spiritual. So let's get on with the joy of living. You know you're not alone. All you have to do is reach out and listen.

MEDITATION

Meditation is what are you thinking about today. What color are your thoughts. Are you green with envy? Red with anger? Or are you trying to change your thinking? What is a thought? A thought is energy. Energy is light. Emotion. I never knew I thought. As one man asked me, "What is mind?" I said, "I don't know, but I'll find out." So I started studying the Science of Mind. I started studying the Bible. And I hated that Bible. The woes and the wickeds and all these things. I was going to burn in hell. But, spiritual discernment.

I asked Little Boss, "All right, buddy, you're the guy that's got me here. You teach me." Spiritual discernment. So I looked at all the so-called disciples as alcoholics. And this is the way THEY understood God. And I looked at Jesus as something that I didn't understand, but now I do. 'Cause He personalized God's love for us. He married death and showed us we have eternal life.

This is a spiritual room right now 'cause we all should have been dead many years ago. We died many times to get here. The hereafter is right here. You see? And we are waking up to our true nature.

***

If we can only believe that God loves and understands us and accept it, you know. And as I used to say, "I love you, God, whether you love me or not." I always thought I was too unworthy to be loved, but that's a cop out too, you know. When we feel guilty or have false pride, it means we feel superior to God. And poor God, He has a rough time with His alcoholic-drug addict children. We're such rebels.

A thought came to me that if you would just sit for 10 minutes, three times a day - sun up, at noon, and sun down, just with the word LOVE up in your third eye in the middle of your forehead, and looking up - just look up - just look up. And it's a strange feeling that you'll have, and this feeling I get is that you better get out of California. It keeps coming to me so strong, and of course I can't change anything that's going to happen. If you're gonna go, well, I reckon it's time for you to go. But you're not going to get away with anything, 'cause Bob and Bill (founders of AA) will meet you on the next plane of existence, and you'll have to fulfill that which you didn't fulfill here. So, let's get on a plane and get out of there. I'm really serious. This strange feeling I have is that California is really going into the ocean pretty soon.

You know, we know but very little, but God will reveal more to you and to me when we're ready for it. But evidently we can't transmute something that we haven't experienced or lived. God gives us the knowledge, and we live it, and give it, and it turns into wisdom. You're not alone. There are trillions of little birds running around in human ignorance 'cause they won't spend time being quiet. How do you communicate with your fellow man? You talk a little, and listen a little. If you don't listen to Him you don't know what He's saying.

WILLINGNESS

The key of willingness? Well, actually alcohol made me willing. I really didn't have any choice. I have a choiceless awareness now. God doesn't have a choice. But turning our will over to Him is the willing, the emotions and the thoughts (a thought plus a feeling becomes an earth motion - our very body temple.) And the body is the life. Without our body, we wouldn't have life on this planet. So, Step three, we turn our will and our life (our thoughts, emotions and body) over to God as we understand Him.

It's like as we walk up the stairway of AA, how do we know if we've turned our will and life over? It's because we take the Fourth Step. And then the Fifth, Sixth, Seventh, Eighth, Ninth,

Tenth, Eleventh and Twelfth. And as a result of working and trying to live these steps, we awaken to our own spirit within ourselves. Which is a radiant light that is glowing all the time.

How do we know that we've turned our will over? 'Cause we get glimpses of beauty, of peace, of oneness. And the absence of God actually is the presence of God because we never knew there was a God. But turning our will, which is our little ego (some call it the little ego, some call it the false self, some the little self) we turn it over to a higher self, we start transmuting and transforming it into the Godself. We don't really crucify the ego, nor do we retire the ego - the higher self just absorbs the little ego, the little self, the little personality, and uses it as its instrument of love and of life, showing others that if they let go of their old ideas of the body, of the self, of the spirit which we all are, that the high self slowly but surely transmutes and transforms and transfigures this so-called ego of ours into unity.

When we turn our will over to the higher self, over to God, then He starts working through our mental body, emotional body, and physical body, and blending, fusing and balancing it, 'cause God is energy, and we've been unbalanced energy - mostly negative. So, actually, guilt and false pride are the two thieves on the cross. And it's strange how you don't really know what's happening, because the heart is the receiver in meditation. Through meditation the higher energy enters in and starts transforming our body temple.

And love without a price tag is leaving all results to God daily. Learning to clean house and trust God. Cleaning house is checking out, asking, am I trying to give or get? 'Cause the little ego likes to get. It's amazing how all of a sudden you start responding instead of reacting. You can tell when it's the little self, 'cause you react.

We've all had emotional, sensitive feelings, wanting to be people pleasers because of our fear of God, actually, we fear we'll be punished. So, more and more as we try to live these Steps, especially the Seventh, which is humility, knowing we are powerless, and the body starts responding, we find the new energy of love in it, and start responding instead of reacting. And that's one way of knowing that God IS taking over. For me, the last thing to be healed is the body temple 'cause I totally destroyed it. But it, too, is getting healthy now. In another fifteen years, it probably will be perfect. God bless you.

LOVE AND SERVICE

How we do try to step back into our old role because society says it's necessary. Poor ol' society is hittin' bottom. You know, they put up $400,000 a year on the methadone program, and the junkies just turn to methadone instead of heroin, and if they took it away from them, they'd go back to heroin. Kinda sad.

***

God, now I know why I'm here. All these people falling off the program, 'cause they're miserable instead of happy. Humility is the price we pay. Complete defeat in every aspect of our lives. You know, we can't go back. We gotta keep going forward, NO MATTER HOW PAINFUL IT SEEMS TO BE.

We have to learn to love and serve or suffer. Love and serve or suffer. You know, God doesn't want to be served. He doesn't want his feet kissed or washed. He just wants to walk with us hand in hand. He's very, very human, and wants to walk hand in hand livin', lovin', laughin', and being joyous in life and letting life express itself through us.

A guy called last night. He just got in from Alaska, and some gal told him that Flobird was in Hawaii, and she was a bird that flew all over the world without any money. That intrigued him, so he called me and wants to come out and see me and find out what my formula is. Won't he be surprised when I say humility and gratitude - opens all the doors. You know, God provides where He guides. We never really give anything, we're all receivers.

***

Your children have a great understanding, and they are really evolved souls that have been here many times before. And they're here to help humanity awaken. So be of good cheer little bird, and be good to yourself. God is having a hard time being happy on this planet. He really is.

***

So, we that glorify God marvel that from so short a life and from so elementary a practice of meditation we have been able to embrace love and service.

Great love and great suffering are our disciplinarians. We need none other. We have to adhere to the principles of AA, or we sicken and die. For us to drink is to die. For us to think negatively is to die. For us to fail to give is to die. And what have you been giving lately except a bunch of negative emotions. Poor little ol' me? Poor little ol' me.

Have you given a dollar to an old wino today? Have you put your hand out and said, "Hey man, it's gonna get better. Here let me help." No, we go to meetings, and we say, "Oh my God, what a horrible life I have. Nobody loves me. Everybody hates me, I'm going out and eat worms. Great big, fat ones, little, bitty, skinny ones." Huh? So, I am the bird that ate the worm that was me. Let's keep it simple and try to live, love, laugh, and be happy today.

***

More birds are coming to the meetings with open hearts and open minds. Those that rebel can't come around. Kinda neat. Seems like God is dividing the planet into two worlds. As He said, I am the body of the new, and I am the shepherd of the old, and they're both one. Those that are loving and giving are being separated and isolated in unity, so they can establish their heaven here on earth, and those that are still asleep and are rebelling are divided into another world. Because hate and love can't really live in the same house. The joy of good living is the ultimate reality of AA when you do the footwork through humility.

JOY MATES

Today is Tom's sixth year AA birthday, and we're gonna bake him a cake and rejoice with him over his happy, miserable sobriety. He's still seeking the spiritual joy mate, and as I tell him, "Give up seeking, and it will walk in." But he has his measurements and his idea of what she has to look like, and what she has to be like. God may have something more beautiful for him. But at this point in time, he can't trust God to know what a spiritual joy mate is. So, he's gonna have to suffer a little bit longer. But I'm sure that when it's time and he's ready for it, she will fly in. That'll be the day.

He's so beautiful and lovable, but he doesn't think so. He has a negative self image. That's one of the things we have to get rid of, you know. Transmute it. 'Cause guilt is of the emotions, and of course, pride is of the mind. Those are two bugaboos that we have to constantly struggle with. When we feel guilty, we think we're the doer of the action. God works in duality, you know. Negative and positive, balancing His little bodies. So it's about time for me to go to the ocean while the sun is out.

***

I've been trying to finish this tape all week, but God's been keeping me pretty busy. The sunrise was so beautiful this morning. So red, and, ahhh, WOW! It is sooo beautiful here. I just rejoice every day at the beauty.

The convention's going to be November 14, and I really don't know whether I'll be here for it or not, but many people are expected. I led the Narcotics Anonymous meeting last night, and WOW - so much rebellion, you know. They're sure dying hard. It was a good meeting. I kinda poked all these little love vibes at them. So many beautiful girls walking around alone, and beautiful guys walking around alone, and everybody's lonely and can't get together, so be grateful you've got B-. Give yourself a chance to love him without a price tag. Many people are looking for their mate and can't find them. It's like a divided house.

HAWAII - 1973-1974

It's like being on another planet. It REALLY is. The peace and the beauty and the happiness, and I'm just rejoicing. You know, God does give me beautiful surprises. So more will be

Flobird: A Bird's Eye View

revealed. The convention is November 14, the one they have every year here in Hawaii. And if God doesn't send me away too soon, I may be able to go to it. More will be revealed.

***

Hi! It's Flobird, a happy, grateful, alcoholic and drug addict living today ONLY by the grace of God in AA, and that is rigorous honesty. You know, if you ever want to find out where I am, Honey, ask God. He'll tell you if you'll keep the transmitter closed and listen. It was real good to hear from you, and I've been thinking about you.

Hawaii still belongs to me. I've got it in my heart. Let's see now. Hawaii, Hawaii, Hawaii. God made Hawaii His spouse and crowned her with all the jewels of heaven, and gave it to me. And I've got it in my heart, you see. So, really, when you take your walk up the Ala Wai, you should see the beauty, the sparkle of beauty and absorb that into your body form. Change your consciousness, become aware, expand your awareness. See how much light there is. See the little flowers that no one notices. Just lean down, and say hi to them. They are life, and they respond to love. Talk to the trees, and they'll talk back. If your body is weary, lean up against a tree, and it will give you vibrations of energy. 'Cause everything is energy. We live, and move, and have our being in light which is energy in motion. It's so simple.

***

When the day breaks in your heart, you find out that you are life. This is Flobird, a happy, grateful, alcoholic and drug addict living today ONLY by the grace of God in AA, and that's rigorous honesty. You know God gave me a big surprise. He sent me back to my homeland - Hawaii. And it's 90 today with the trade winds blowing, and the palm trees singing. We have white doves in the back yard. We're about two blocks from the beach. The sky is so beautiful and blue. This is truly heaven on earth. I didn't know I was coming here, you know. It's strange how God does arrange things.

I've had a quiet heart and empty think tank ever since I left New Mexico. I was there ten weeks in the magic forest, more or less in silence. The birds are all working hard preparing for the winter. It was getting really cold when Tom said, "Hey Flobird, you're going with me to California." And I said, "Oh, O.K. Why not." So we spent a week in California and arrived here last week, and it's really beautiful. Many hearts are open right now.

I had forgotten how beautiful Hawaii was. I try to stay detached. It took God ten years to really detach me from here. And I haven't been here for a year and a half, and I thought "mission accomplished". No more coming back. So, it's like I say, God made Hawaii His spouse, and crowned her with all the jewels of heaven and gave her to me. And I become willing to let it go, and I get to come back for about a minute. I don't know how long I'll be here. But as long as I'm here, I'm really enjoying it. To wake up in the warmth. Golly, it's heavenly. It really is. It's like I'm on another planet.

We're going into Scorpio now which is the beginning of some new lessons and the ending of some old. So hang loose, and flow with it.

VIRGINIA BEACH - 1973

We've all gone and had our etheric bodies sealed, so we won't pick up all the negative energy. When you get here, I'm gonna take you to Dr. Whitehouse, 'cause I imagine you got quite a few holes in your etheric body from all your drinking and your stinking thinking. It's really neat. 'Cause this body of mine is really getting so healthy and so young, I'll have to start looking for a spiritual joy mate pretty soon. That'll blow everybody's mind. Well, just for today, I think I'm gonna take a nap before the meeting.

We had quite a meeting yesterday. There were about 40 little birds here. All wanting to learn to live, love, laugh and be happy.

The weather here is so strange. It's like a heat that I've never experienced before. There's not a breath of air. It's about 92. We're very fortunate to have an air conditioner in the house, yet we got our electric bill, and it was $206 for last month, so the electric company is really making money on this hot weather.

My heart tells me to stay here. Although I'm getting a pull to go to Hawaii, I think it's Tom wanting me to come over, so I have to listen real close to my heart to find out what God really wants me to do. So, just for today, the joy of living, of good living, is the ultimate reality of AA. May God bless you and keep you little one.

***

Thinking about our relationship for the eight or nine years, and reflecting on how every time this bag of bones of mine got so tired giving love for hate, you always appeared and took me home and took care of me. And it's been wonderful, really. I just want to thank you for loving me for the many times you've helped me keep on this path of return. So, thank you, dear one, for loving me and always being there when I really needed you.

ASSOCIATION FOR RESEARCH AND ENLIGHTENMENT 1976-77: PAST LIVES, REGRESSIONS

Casey's center has many people flocking there. They have every spiritual book in their library that's ever been written. It's the most fabulous library, and they have a book store that has any spiritual book you could possibly want covering all religions. And they have psychic readers there, too. Casey's secretary is still alive. She's about 80 years old. They have someone in Virginia Beach who's an astrologer and can regress you back consciously, so you can remember everything. Takes you right back through your past life.

One of the birds was regressed, and he was on this island. He said, "I'm 20 and I'm sitting on the beach." It was Seashell Island off of Africa, I believe it was, and he was there all alone until he was 80 years old. That's when he died. But, five people visited the island from England, and he recognized one of them as someone he knew in this life. He fell in love with her, but he didn't get her. She left. And this is the way it's been in this life. She has been his only love, and he's always saying good bye to her and putting her on planes. It's fantastic.

He was taken out of his body, and when he was leaving his body he was asked, "Now tell me what does your body look like?"

"It's an old body lying there in a thatched shack that I lived in, and I was alone all those years." A lonely life.

As his spirit body was leaving, he was asked, "What did you learn in this life, and what do you see now?"

"I am looking over the earth, and I see many people that need to be loved. I learned I must go back to earth and learn about God and help people."

You can even get under the hypnosis of this man's voice on the tape. He is so beautiful.

I had a reading with Joy, our little psychic medium, not too long ago, and in some of my past lives, I was a slave, a gypsy, and the greatest thing was that I was Simon Peter with Jesus. You know, the one that denied him three times? And, it could be, you know. It ain't no big thing, because it's what are we doing NOW. Are we trying to become one with our Godself. 'Cause that's the most important thing in our lives today; to let the spirit take over mental, emotional, physical, and become free to be ourselves.

I was just reminded of why I keep on smoking. When I asked God to release me from this obsession, burning tobacco fields came to my head, and I asked Joy about it. And she picked up I did burn tobacco fields in Kentucky in one of my past lives. It was like the Klu Klux Klan. I was against smoking, therefore, I played God, and took it into my own hands and purged all these people. I took away their livelihood which was tobacco, so why should God remove my obsession until I've suffered enough or at least with as much suffering as I've caused.

When we understand the law of Karma, it's really lessons that are unlearned, and when we turn our will and life over to God, we turn our Karma over to Him, and He works it out for us through loving action. When we're willing to accept all the crap, all the hate, and all the suffering we put out, we fulfill it, or He fulfills it for us in a very few years. Watch your thinkin' little one. No more stinkin' thinkin' - Okay?

Flobird: A Bird's Eye View

***

God's taking His Sixth, Seventh, Eighth and Ninth Steps on the whole planet, so we can turn around, reach for the stars and climb the ladder, or we can dip into the bottomless pit. Once we leave this planet in this century, if we haven't really become pure in heart and opened our minds to pure reason, I don't believe we'll be able to come back for 1,000 years. Until the planet is established in love wisdom, 'cause this is our second solar system, and it's called love wisdom. Isn't that intersting? There is so much to learn. Golly, it's like I live under a cloud of unknowing and forgetting.

So, get you a crystal ball, little one. Crystal is pure energy. Then look into it, and become one with all life, Okay? All the energy you spend on being miserable and wanting to die and self centeredness. Man, look what you could do if you used it constructively. You know a bird takes no thought for its life, it takes thought for other people's lives. A bird rises upon its wings of love and service above the mental hate of man. It doesn't depend on a tree. It depends on its wings. A bird is a very spiritual thing, so don't knock the birds. They can fly.

***

You know our universe contains many worlds for our souls to inhabit, and after we are passed on to other universes, there will still be infinity before us. There are now many souls in existence on planes infinitely higher than our own intelligence of transcendent glory and magnificence. And they were once men even as we are today. There is no limit to our progression towards all perfection.

So, little one, you're gonna live forever ascending to higher and higher planes, and then on, and on, and on. And as we progress on to higher planes of life, we shall incarnate in bodies far more ethereal or spiritual than those that are now used by us. Just as in the past, we used bodies almost incredibly grosser and coarser than those we call our own today.

FLYING SAUCERS EXTRATERRESTRIALS

I'm studying about other worlds now, and other tongues,

and other flesh, and the flying saucers which are really spiritual beings trying to balance this universe, so man with his hate and his hostility and defiance doesn't blow it up. It's been a little nip and tuck the last ten years. We nearly blew ourselves up. Like the planet Lucifer - it blew itself up trying to take over the solar system, and now I think it's an asteroid belt, and some of its meteorites hit our planet, and we transform them, too.

You know our flying saucers are really spiritual beings, spiritual intelligence who were human beings like we are, or they still may be, only they have progressed to other grandeurs. They still have a long way to go, as we do. And our saucer intelligence tells us, we are all sons of God, and the plan is to be the abode of man. The human form and the human race are universal. They are our wonderful brothers and sisters, and they told us that what we had hoped was true before the dawn of history, that life is eternal, that we are immortal beings, so why don't you believe it? These space people are offering their brothers of earth the wonderful eternal gifts of great value, so let us in all humbleness accept what they have to offer, and thank our infinite Father for sending them to us at this time instead of trying to shoot them down.

'Cause the time is getting shorter, and we have but a little while to choose, for it is written: The harvest shall be removed on the day of inheritance. Help has come from outer space for millions of years to try to bring us health and peace and abundant joy, but we wouldn't have it until we suffered enough. 'Cause the people on earth are starving for truth, so let us help them to find the light that is within themselves. We are still a little child, and we want to tear apart everything that is, to see what makes it tick.

You know, I was going to call the scientists when I was watching TV, and they were wondering if there was life on Mars. Good heavens to Betsy, life is all there really is. And many of the Mars people live underground because of the heat. And the spacemen from Mars have been coming to our planet for many years, and all these little red, blue, white and yellow balls that we've seen all over the earth planet actually are fire balls that are rejuvenating our earth 'cause man has taken out all of its life, so they're putting life back in to it. When man awakens and opens his mind and gets rid of his false pride, he will awaken to the cosmic rays that are hitting our planet to keep it balanced.

Beautiful things are happening because we are moving into a warmer climate. The whole universe is moving into another area of space. Isn't that intersting? Life is fascinating, Little One. Wake UP! Become aware that God, if you want to call it God, is everywhere because life is everywhere. You can't escape it. Darkness is only the absence of light, so everything can sleep. You need to sleep, and life and death are one. Death is like going to sleep at night and waking up in the morning. Let us die unto all our old ideas and awaken to the new ones, Okay? Since we're traveling Northward, and when the earth turns on its axis and starts Southward again, this area will be the West.

***

The number 4 in numerology is harmony, truth, and conflict - the number of humanity. This is the last weekend for all of the people in Virginia Beach. We'll have a ghost town next week. Everybody will go home. Only a few restaurants will be open. And it will be kinda neat. All that vibration will leave Virginia Beach, and we'll be peaceful and more will be revealed. I reckon it's been a good season for the restaurants but not as good as last year.

A doctor from Virginia Beach went to Kansas to speak revealing the secrets of mother nature and color healing. It's time now to bring it out so the doctors, psychiatrists and scientists will awaken. And they can't crucify him now. That is past. There are so many spiritual beings protecting those of us that live for love and service and new ideas. No man can tear us apart now and hang us on a cross. I'm so grateful that the dark time of the karma of the planet is over, and we're all ascending. Now, if man tries to crucify another man, he dies in his own vomit. It's really neat.

REBELLION

Good morning Birds. This is Flobird, a happy, grateful alcoholic and drug addict rebelling today against God. I called Him a phony. And said that He was very cruel, and He delighted in using us like pin balls, you know, in a bowling alley? He knocks us down, and then stands us up, and then knocks us down again. I always go through this when one of the birds are hurting, and their faith is challenged. And I know it's good, very, very good.

Anyway, this morning, all of a sudden, I was telling God what a rotten world He has and how rotten and decayed and depraved humanity was, and the whole ball of wax hit me. Every once in a while, especially when one of the birds is going through the deepest wound of the soul, I get that spirit rebellion again. He said "It's gotta get worse before it gets better. Only the pure in heart can enter the Kingdom of Heaven." But Good God!

You know, I can see the duality of God. The cruel God that would go to any length to sacrifice a part of Him for the good of the whole. And the weak shall inherit the earth cause when you're weak, all the strong wants to help you. The weak eats up the strong's energy and becomes strong itself. That's why the weakest link in the chain of sobriety in AA is the strongest, because you see, everyone gives the sick, weak, little alcoholic their strength. They say they're not ready, but then they take off with all that energy of love, and misuse it again, through ignorance, through their own karma.

But it's like up in New Mexico when Marchand was suffering so, and MAN, I went into one of these, "God, You're a phony, and You go to any length to crucify Yourself." So, I had my time of rebellion this morning, and went out and sat by the bay and started laughing. The Cosmic Mad Man is right. And I could see God as so powerless. He is so powerless. He set the ball rolling 21 million years ago, and He's got to accept the things He cannot change, the cycles He put Himself through, and we share in Christ's sufferings as well as His blessings.

But HOLY MACKEREL, Man, you know. I was ready to go

Flobird: A Bird's Eye View

out and get my whip, and beat up all these perverted, cruel pieces of energy who are running around eating up my doves. Oh God. Man. Well, you know, great love and great suffering are our disciplinarians. And, God does deal the cards, but gee whiz, sometimes I just want to hit Him over the head. And so, we walk on.

I met a delightful lady next door. Her husband died a couple of months ago. She believes in the universal mind. I believe she's Jewish, so called. She's a delight. She starts rapping to me, and I said, "Well, don't you believe in life after death?" And she said, "Oh, no! I don't want any more!"

And she cannot believe she'll see her husband again. So I took her *Love from Eternity* to read. She looked at me and said, "I don't believe it. You disarm me every time you talk to me. But you give me faith that there are good people in the world." So, I thought, well, you gotta keep believin' that there are. You gotta keep believin' that God is love and all good. If you don't, you're lost.

JUDGMENT

It's so simple to get sucked into the cesspool of humanity. Especially when you're trying to love without judgment, without being the jury, the judge, and executioner of your fellow man.

That's why AA is such a protective mantle around us. Who are we to judge anybody else, 'cause we've done it all, you know. Not in this life. Past lives. Oh God, you know, we do get caught in that vibration. We are so powerless. Which is showing you how powerless our loving God is. He suffers right with us. As I told Him this morning, that divine impersonal God that steps on us little ants of humanity for the good of the whole is just gotta, gotta STOP, you know. CRUSH, CRUSH. GRIND, GRIND. Stand up and do it again. Boy, I was just spittin' fire this morning.

And Cherie kinda jerked around, and looked at me. And I said "It's a rotten, rotten world! Rotten humanity! God's a phoney!" Then I went outside. It's all a divine comedy.

I can understand so much. Jesus on the cross or God of

love on the cross saying, "Forgive them. They know not what they're doing." 'Cause they really don't. They don't know how powerless they are to be sucked into this vibration of hate. That's why it's so difficult for anyone to come back into AA, and also so difficult for those in AA to find this pearl of great price right now. The cycle of time has sped up so much.

I can feel people's death wish. This is the great love and great suffering. I suffer with those souls that are waking up and seeing how powerless they are over the so called evil of the world. The darkness of the world. So, all we can do is stand, pray and watch, kick our feet, rebel like hell, and walk on.

From our joy comes our sorrow. From our sorrow comes our joy. And it is so true. But there is a permanent joy, and there is a permanent high. And no matter what falls down outta the sky or what comes up outta the earth, there is that oneness that cannot be shaken, and it cannot be taken away from us. I've proven it over and over again.

And today, going back within myself to understand the deep hurt of Cherie, I relived my life with Milt for three and a half years. He was my personal love in AA, and I knew that God would heal him and his Christ self would come out, and we would live happily ever after. Every time he would bring me a big bouquet of roses, then he would pick up a drink the next day, bring home a playboy magazine with beautiful girls in it and say, "I'd rather masturbate and look at these girls than go to bed with you." It broke my heart. Every time. Until the body was completely worn out. The emotions. I could cry no more tears of hurt. It was something else. And every time he'd hit a bottom, God would send me back to him. And he'd sober up on sex which was the most grueling experience I've had, but the results are that today he is alive and being used constructively.

But, oh, my God, it is something else! We all seek that joy mate. Then we find out we are our own joy mate, and find complete release from all transitory joy mates. And I know that each and every one of you birds will find your mate, physically, in the form. I'm just one that God has picked to walk with Him alone, I reckon, 'cause I wouldn't know what to do with one at this point in time. He'd probably flip out. Any hoo, I am very grateful I am here to walk through this with Cherie. Now I know why He kept me here instead of sending me to Hawaii. He knew this was coming. And it's like I live under the cloud of unknowing, the cloud of forgetting. And this too shall pass away.

Perfect light changing form. Oh yeah, I have switched to Carlton cigarettes. It's like switching from hard liquor to beer. Man, I eat up two packs in six hours. It's kind of ridiculous, really. But here, again, I'm powerless over it. I feel like going out and getting some Camels. Go out and really get it on. Why play with it. All these little dilemmas. The greatest thing that AA teaches us is to quit taking ourselves so damn serious, and when we fall down, humility picks us up, and we laugh at ourselves. Laugh, clown, laugh.

I'll probably go to a meeting today. They will say, "I thought you went to Hawaii?" "Oh, God changed his mind," I'll answer. "You know, He doesn't really know what He's doing."

All the people around here look at us, and they really don't know how to take us. 'Cause truth changes in the moment, as long as we're maintaining good-natured flexibility, and MAN we have to today to keep up with this divine flux, that says do it, no, don't do it, do it. We have to stay in constant silence within ourselves to pick up what God is trying to tell us. That still small voice. 'Cause, He isn't quite sure which way humanity is gonna jump. All He can do is keep on tryin', and I can see it so plain.

I can't really put it in words. All our dreams are coming true. The vision is so beautiful. But it's like walking through the human scene. Being neutral you know. Just keep on lovin'. It's very ticklish. It's very dangerous. In a moment you could be snuffed out or you could live forever - there's no human words that can describe the chaos, the erratic energy that's dancing around in the planet today. It's fascinating. And I'm grateful to be part of it, but also to fall free of all of it.

And sometimes you fly through these two rockets comin' at you, and you either duck under, go over, or go between them, and then you look back and think, "Oh, my God." It's like dropping the atomic bomb at Hiroshima. Only God knew what Karma that created in the universe. And it's all coming back to us.

It isn't punishment. It's lessons. To teach all humanity to love each other without judgment. Not to try to manipulate or mentally judge or try to control anybody's life, even our own. To leave it to a Higher Power. We do live in the heart of the sun 'cause this planet is the Christ-love planet, and God is turning all his scars into stars right here on this planet.

Love is healing all the wounds of experience that we dare to walk through, and is taking on the suffering, so it can be transmuted within a shorter time. And there will come that time when God will wipe away every tear of our eyes, and we will run and not be weary, and we will fly like eagles in the sky, and we WILL march together in equality, loving each other and rejoicing in life eternal.

It IS coming, and we MUST have faith. We must have blind faith at times knowing it's good, very, very good. Yes, we must keep on keeping on. Faith is truly the substance of all things hoped for, the evidence of things not seen. But when you can see the glorious vision that's ahead for us, there is nothing that can get you down for very long. The very earth is moaning and groaning to be free. It is coming. It is coming.

So let's all be joyous warriors, and take love as our sword and keep giving love for hate. That's the greatest gift. Humility is the healer of all pain. To be grateful for our pain, 'cause it's God Himself suffering.

***

I'm not coughing as much. (Cough) See? And I just chewed up another pack of cigarettes, and I have one more pack left. You know how Cherie rebels against buying me cigs. I think it's more because she knows it's trying to annihilate this body more than the green energy she's spending, 'cause now, she's back in that same spot of, "Oh my God, how will I make the rent payment?" This too shall pass away.

So, all you little birds. I love you, and love never gives up. There's no hopeless human being. Sooner or later they're gonna have to wake up and become willing to live instead of die.

***

The song DAYBREAK, I just love it! 'Cause that's what's happening, you know. Humanity's heart center is awakening and everybody is trying to wake up and do good, and truly the New Age is coming, unfolding.

No man can judge another man in this New Age 'cause it only comes back to him and it destroys him. And if you see that counselor that's always talking against the birds, tell him he's next if he doesn't quit judging. Tell him he's not hurting anybody but himself. But he can't help it, you know. That's undoubtedly the lessons he came here to learn - that no man can judge another man. In God's eyes we're all equal. No superior or inferior. Just each one expressing life uniquely. And as we find our unique talents, we use them for the good of the whole and fly free. Funzee.

We are going into Scorpio which is the testing period. Hang loose and walk through this balancing of the negative energy within our bodies. Rejoice in the struggle. The struggle is the journey. Coming to that point where we don't have to struggle anymore; it does happen. We just keep practicing love, and humility which is loving without judgment, and who are we to be judge, jury and executioner of our fellowman? That's a big burden.

So, give everybody my love, darling, and quit fighting anything or anybody. We have to in order to live. As I told God the other night, You know, I'm not gonna go now unless I can take my body with me. That's a far cry from trying to destroy the body and get off this planet.

So, give all your children my love, and some hugs, and some pats. I wrote Neil and Beth. I reckon they're in the Virgin Islands about now. Just finished Neil Hancock's fourth book. And I wish there was another one. 'Cause it's what's happening right now, and as he said, the light, love, peace, and joy will win out. So, Aloha and God bless you.

***

Living is giving love. And love is unlimited. It cannot be expressed in anything except giving, and you cannot pinpoint love 'cause God is love, so let's get on with this life that's unfolding so beautifully. Every little soul is unfolding its own pattern, and no man can judge another man. We are in the new age now. And no man can judge in this new age, 'cause it's instant Karma returned. Karma means action in living. So, there's so much beauty around you if you'll just turn your eyeballs outward instead of inward and be grateful. Takes many humiliations to find a degree of humility. And humility is knowing there's a power greater than ourselves running this universe.

FEAR

Fear of rejection is what makes us overeat, oversmoke, oversex, overdrink. Fear of not being loved. So, we start trying to love that self and fill that lonely o' vacuum that's in our hearts.

Trying to help people face life with joy instead of fear, 'cause fear is the corroding thread that keeps us from living, loving, laughing, and being happy.

And what do we fear? God, we've been through death so many times. I saw a program on TV yesterday about death education, and it's really great. A rabbi (he was so beautiful, this rabbi) said that at the first death education, you go and bathe and purify the dead body, and you have to touch it and hold it, and purify it with water. He said even though he's a rabbi, a man of God, he really didn't want to touch the body. But that's what's happening. They're starting this death education in schools in Minneapolis, and it's far out.

Everybody has been fearing death. You know, I gotta do this before I die, so they forget to live 'cause they're meditating on death. And, as we know, there is no death except like going to sleep at night and waking up to a new world in the morning. Many birds here that are waking up, and their hearts are open, taking their Fourth and Fifth Steps, and coming alive.

***

Just for today my heart is very quiet, empty think tank, so I reckon I'll be here today. The doves are singing my love songs,

Flobird: A Bird's Eye View

and the beautiful Plumeria flowers smell so good. A letter from the birds in New Mexico. It's 28 degrees at night and about 60 in the day, so it's pretty cold. We had rain yesterday. And the waves are about 8-14 feet high. Ocean is so blue and beautiful. 'Course, this is my homeland. It would be nice to stay here all winter, but I belong to God, and He uses me wherever He pleases.

ALCOHOL AND DRUGS

One of my birds that had been sober quite awhile relapsed into our disease and started taking Dexedrine which is speed, and became a speed freak. I told her to go to the AA meeting last night, and she said, "Well, I'm not a drug addict," and I said, "What else do you think you are?" God, people here just can't see that alcohol is a narcotic in liquid form, and she quit drinking when she started taking speed. Then she got hooked on it and was well on her way to becoming a full-blown hard-core heroin addict 'cause from speed comes the needle and cocaine... and a lot of cocaine and heroin running around here.

False pride's a killer, you know. I'm not like that, they say. So we keep on keepin' on, planting seeds, trying to help people.

RESERVATIONS

I rejoiced when you told me J- picked up a drink. Now maybe he'll either wake up dead or come alive.

There's so many that have been so miserable sober, 'cause they don't want to be alcoholics, and they think it's a punishment to have to go to AA, but it really takes what it takes to wake up that AA is a spiritual underground to lead us to freedom. Freedom of the human spirit just to be ourselves, you know. And God does work in duality. Negative and positive. God is life changing form constantly. His will is to live, love, laugh and be happy.

SURRENDER

So, it's very simple. Very simple. And you might as well surrender, totally surrender 'cause you're gonna have to anyway. You know you've surrendered to misery, and you're so busy being unhappy that you can't see the forest for the trees. But, not a soul shall be lost. So, if you don't make it on this planet, you're gonna make it on another one, and you're gonna take your consciousness with you 'cause our consciousness is God within. And if you haven't improved your conscious contact, then baby, you're just circling in your own orbit repeating your experiences 'till you learn your lesson.

The Cosmic Lord looks upon us, but He helps us and can't really take our little will. It was free in the beginning. God provided, and we divided through selfishness. So until we voluntarily give our little will with complete abandon to a Higher Power, we just keep on having a little peace, but not all the peace, we have a little love, but not all our love. Love can only fulfill itself. Love will not possess or be possessed. Love just keeps on keepin' on. And the greatest, most beautiful things are happening.

Earth changes are happening. We're becoming aware of the earthquakes all over. Where there's negative energy, there is going to be earthquakes, and there's gonna be tidal waves over this whole planet. And you can commit legal suicide by going where the earthquake faults are if you don't want to stay here any longer. But all is being revealed. We have eternal life. If we don't make it here, we're gonna make it somewhere else. All that we have will be given. Someday it shall all be given. So we might as well give now. Okay?

Be of good cheer. Out of the heart comes the issues of life, and in the heart lurks the evil of man. And what is the evil but negative energy, lack of trust, lack of faith. We have more faith in our little selves than we have in the one of whom it can be said has been running the solar system for billions of years. It's all a divine comedy. The human being has no power. It's the light within that doeth all the works.

Flobird: A Bird's Eye View

POWERLESSNESS

It hasn't been easy. I've been trying to kick cigarettes. And I'll tell you it's harder than kicking alcohol. This morning I woke up, and I had made a stop date - May 1st. I will give up cigarettes. I've read books on it like I did on everything else. How to do it. I read books last year on it. My two daughters read and quit smoking. I read books four times, kept smoking. This book I just finished. Made a stop date. Today I'm not going to smoke. So I took all my cigarettes and everything (my paraphernalia) and give 'em to my daughter. Said, "I quit!"

I woke up for meditation and sat there for about an hour, and all I could meditate on was I want a cigarette. I want a cigarette. I am so powerless over it. And it brought to mind how powerless I was when I came here. Powerlessness is something I kicked against all my life. Powerless to make people know I existed. Powerless as a rebel all my life. Rebelling against everything anybody told me 'cause I knew it wasn't true. I was a juvenile delinquent. I was a non-conformist. I was all these things. Then I found alcohol. I loved it. And I still love it today. 'Cause it allowed me to dance and romance and do the things I wanted to do. But I didn't have the courage to do them sober. I was one that ran from violence. And ran from domineering people. I admired my sister so much 'cause she could cut people to pieces with her tongue, and I couldn't. I'd just stand there and cry. Then I'd go home and say, "I should have said this."

Now, today, I'm very grateful I was a self hater. You know, I can't judge anybody or anything. I can't even judge the guy that murders 'cause I murdered myself.

Now I can see that I came alive. I started coming alive. And it wasn't easy. I still have a subtle death wish. That's why I keep smoking. Keep hanging onto that. Maybe I can get out of here pretty soon.

I was talking to a bird the other day, and he said, "Well, how can I get the peace and permanent high that you've got?" I said, "Well, let go with complete abandon. You know, if your job bugs you, let it go. If your house bugs you, let it go. My world is not of your world." He started rebelling. He didn't realize what I meant is my world that I live in today is full of love, and peace, and joy, and understanding, and compassion. My world isn't the world of the old ideas I had of God, of life, of myself and of people. That's the old world. It stopped and let me off, and I don't want back on it. And I go to any length not to get back on it.

I have taken my hat and walked out of the house and slept on the beach because the turmoil in the house was gettin' to me. Humility is our guide. Complete abandon. You see, I did anything drunk. I do anything sober. The thing I fear to do, I do it, and it turns into faith. And it isn't me doing it. It takes guts to stay sober. Anybody can pick up a drink.

AA is a very simple program. Very difficult though, 'cause it does take pain to grow spiritually. And rebellion does dog our very footsteps. It's like fighting this cigarette here. I am powerless over it, and I hate it because I can't throw it away. Powerlessness. I have a choiceless awareness today that is freedom. In my heart I'm free. I can stand on my own two feet in front of the whole multitudes and say, God loves me. God is love. God takes the rejects of the world and builds us up and shows us what His glory can be. By loving each other without judgment.

You see, we can't judge in AA because if we do, we go get drunk. Or we get plunged into mental turmoil and experience an emotional drunk. And you vomit up the vile stuff just like when you're drunk. I didn't know what an emotional drunk was until I went on one. Man, it's worse than getting drunk. A mental drunk is when you have such headaches that you can't do anything. You feel like you're going to explode. A mental drunk. An emotional drunk. We're very fortunate. 'Cause alcohol is patient, and so is God. He's got us right here.

Eternal life. This God didn't give us 70 years in order to accomplish all these things. We've had many bodies before. It's called reincarnation. Rebirth. Call it what you will. It's true, you see. These are the things that I have been given to help people wake up and quit being afraid of death. Quit being afraid of God. Quit being afraid of ourselves. Our stinking thinking. We can get rid of it through humility.

I've watched old timers pick up a drink. I've watched old timers start smoking pot. I've watched them pick up drugs. Why? Two-steppin'. Come to a meeting, I'm an alcoholic, what I used to be like. Come to a meeting. I love ever' one of 'em, and they hate my guts because I'm a happy, grateful alcoholic. One of them said the other night, "I don't see anything to be grateful about." Baby, gratitude is reverence for life. And I didn't have any for 42 years. I had reverence for death. You couldn't scare me to death.

And even these cigarettes. The doctor told me two months ago I had emphysema, and my right lung was collapsing. If I don't give up these cigarettes, I'll die. Do I give them up? I keep smoking. I keep coughing. You can't scare an alcoholic. That's why we're totally insane. But I have accepted my insanity. You tell a normal person, hey, you're gonna die. They give up the cigarettes. Alcoholics of our type can never drink again. We are like men who have lost both legs. They'll never grow new ones in this life. We have to either sober up, flip our lids permanently, or go to the next plane of existence. Bill and Bob are waiting for you. So, you thought you were going to get away with it, huh? We might as well do it in the here and now.

THERE IS A SOLUTION

These are the days when the lion will lie down with the lamb, and God will wipe away every tear from our eyes, and we'll all be called Children of Light going around, and soon there won't be any night, so come on Little bird, ruffle up your wings and take flight, 'cause you too can fly, if you'd just keep it simple and look up at the sky instead of down at the ground.

And quit going around moping. O.K.? Get with those that are full of joy and laughter, and join in with the joyous celebration of the freedom of man. Freedom to be yourself. Freedom to speak when you want to speak, and be silent when you want to be silent. Free to love without judgment. Free just to be a little spirit in the garment of flesh fulfilling your own soul development. If you feel like it, cut the cord on all those things there and fly over here and get a new lease on life.

You know, if you got drunk, you'd do it. You don't have to go get drunk. You got a way up and out. There IS a solution. But you gotta LIVE that solution. And it's in the Big Book and the Twelve and Twelve. This is the way we recover. Deflation of that ego at depth. It takes what it takes. So, you can join us on this beautiful exciting path that we're on, 'cause you do have a way up and out if you want to make the effort. The only mistake we ever make is not learning from our mistakes.

***

Aloha, this is Flobird, a happy, grateful, alcoholic and drug addict living today only by the grace of God in AA, and that's rigorous honesty. Rigorous honesty is freedom. I of myself can do nothing. It's God that keeps me sober. God got me sober. God as I understand him. Self knowledge never kept me sober, but it's the knowledge of God that keeps me sober. And where do we find that knowledge? Well, first things first, we find it in the Big Book and the Twelve and Twelve. And that's the springboard that springs us out to study the Bible which is actually the story of humanity which is us. The Gita, The Hindu Bible and Yoga, the five paths of Yoga, you study the lives of the Saints. They all knew God. And you study your own life.

You're what I used to be like when I tried suicide. I had no purpose for living. You know that's the selfishness of us. We'd rather die than share our life with others, so I think it's about time to take the Fifth Step in AA and quit trying to manage your life and accept that your a little self-will is runnin' riot, and tryin' to find an easier softer way.

That Fourth Step is not a punishing step. It opens the many doors within us. The AA book opens the many mansions within ourselves. It is the first step to open the first door to find out who we are, what we are, and where we're going. How wonderful we really are. We alcoholics are wonderful, lovable, beautiful people. We have lived life to the fullest. We have dared death. We have defied death to the extreme.

For me it was purely humiliating. Take a big overdose of pills and be pronounced dead, and wake up three days later.

And the Doc says, "WHY are you trying to die?" and I say, "I want out of hell!" That's when he told me I either had to go back to Patton State Hospital or take up golf. I took up golf. And I stayed sober for two years playing golf.

AA is a lot like golf. You have to hit your own ball. You have to improve your own game. Nobody can do it for you. It's a discipline game, and I loved it. But it was obsessive. I even took the girls and my husband. They HAD to take up golf. So I wouldn't feel guilty leaving home all the time. Then I lost a tournament and picked up a drink. That's when I went on my last drunk - a nine month drunk. I lost all my beautiful friends.

You know, evolution has sped up. No longer can you go to meetings and live off the other guy's spiritual energy. You've got to generate your own through prayer and meditation. That's why so many are getting drunk and getting on pot. They haven't done their own footwork.

Humanity has taken everything out of the earth and has not given it back anything. So Mother Nature is taking it back herself. In a twinkling of an eye you can turn and say, "Hey God, forgive me for misusing Your creative energy." Get down on your bony knees and your mental knees, and see how puny your idea of life is, how puny man's idea of life is. God will touch you with His little finger, and you will be lifted up and all shall be revealed.

PAIN IS THE TOUCHSTONE

Flobird never let a little pain stop her from sharing with her "birds." She even shared the pain she felt, and she was always hopeful that her body would heal itself.

You know Little One, you are more stabilized in your emotions. Oh dear, everybody is going around trying to stabilize their emotions whereas I just give mine all away. It's like my God is very emotional. He moves in passion and then He's calm. It's pretty wonderful.

When everyone accepts their humanity, which is being

human, you know, it's very simple. And, as for me coming to the VA hospital, Man, they'd never let me out of there. If they ever looked at this body of mine, they'd say, 'It's impossible! Let's put her away!' Thanks for the sweet invitation. All we have to do is be an able example of Jesus' teachings which is to love each other without judgment. Love each other without a price tag. Love each other with joy, joy, joy, joy. So, be of good cheer, Little Bird.

Sorry to hear you're going to buy a house in California. California, you know, is due to go into the ocean at any time, so you'll be buying dead property. But, of course, if you want to commit legal suicide, that's okay too. Can't change what's already happened. I've been telling you that for ten years. As you're going down with the tidal wave, you'll say, 'Oh, that's what Flobird meant'. But that's all right. You'll come up on the other side and see that the only thing that you took with you is what you gave away. We do have eternal life, right now.

***

The body temple seems to be getting a little better. I still have my pain suit on. It all seems to be in my right shoulder, and when I went to an acupuncturist in Grants, New Mexico, he took X-rays and said my bones were luminous. They were so thin you could crack me on the neck and break it. My bones in my body are so fragile. It seems that the body is slowly but surely deteriorating from alcoholism. One of those good things that happens, you know, when we've drunk too long, too much.

So, it will take a miracle of God again to restore it to sanity. I've had 61 good years on this planet, but I reckon God does have a lot more work for me to do. Said I'd be here another 20 years, so that's neat. I'll be here when the reconstruction begins and everybody is livin', lovin', laughin' and being happy which will be within 15 years, and that will be neat.

God put me in a beautiful space to experience all my pain. The body has quit resisting the pain, and is accepting it. You know, our bodies are wonderful. They adjust to just about anything. Birds in Texas sent me some medication. Some kind of stuff for emphysema, and it's helping.

All in all the Bird Group has really progressed and proven

the AA principles. The joy of good living is the ultimate reality of AA.

Cherie wrote a follow up on my 1970 article about the birds, about our Beachcombers Spiritual Progress Group. It will be in the June issue. Next month, I reckon.

There are those that can't seem to stay sober in this life time. They may have to come back again. It will be another 1,000 years before they'll be able to get on this planet again. That's why so many are trying to fulfill their karma in this life time.

It takes all kinds to reach all kinds of minds, so we do follow our heart and not our head. If you see your friend, tell him that long-legged, long-haired spiritual person is still doing her thing.

Better stop now. I'm runnin' out of breath. See you in the morning sun. I love you.

***

Hi birds. Just had a session with a bird in automatic writing. This is what she got yesterday from the spirits: Karma must be worked out between you and Flobird. Love and honesty. Love without a price tag as you call it. We are your spirit guides here to help you. Do not fear. We will be here daily at 7:30. Just let yourself go. Never spend more than 10 minutes a day with us in writing. It is draining now for you. Should be precise on the time we meet. Then we will have a better flow of energies. Flobird will be with you only through your first week of automatic writing. This is all for now.

That's what she got yesterday. And this morning, it was really neat 'cause she even opened her eyes and everything. They said: Good morning. It is time for the awakening of Hawaii. Meaning, the consciousness of people here. A lot of turmoil with locals. You won't be venturing past this house for too long at one time. Establishing a center here at this house temporarily. The next month will be before Fall. Start looking for the land. Time moves quickly for you people. Here on this side, we watch people full of soul pain; in order to awaken, must first come tragedy. Be prepared for an earth change nearby. Do you understand the mental mind of man is the destroyer of this planet. (God, that's so true, said Flobird). You must start replacing all positive thoughts of your own with positive thoughts of others. You are a transmuter and trying to back away from people's energies won't help. So sit quietly in your time of discomfort and bless the people. It's called transmuting energy.

Flobird is in a very hard initiation. We cannot touch her except to say she will know what to do in the moment. Body is human. Accepting that humanity totally will relieve some pressure. Soul is the master. The body is the servant. Yet on earth the soul is also a servant to the body. And that's so true.

Just finished listening to my favorite TV minister. It was so beautiful. Especially on color TV. Listen and glisten. Be a light unto this troubled world. People walk with hurting feet and hurting hearts. Soul hurts, soul wounds. To be a light unto the world. Another thing I heard was learn to grow instead of blow. In other words you can either light a candle or blow it out through your negative thoughts.

It's time for me to take a little nap. I love to go to sleep 'cause then my body doesn't hurt. But this too shall pass away when it's time. So, I'll talk to you later. God loves you, and so do we!

***

I went through quite a crisis yesterday. I woke up dreaming somebody was dragging me by the neck. I felt like I was being dragged, tortured, as if somebody was trying to get me to commit suicide, and I was crawling, and I kept saying, I will not crawl before you. Anyway, it was far out. I went in and I grabbed this bird's hands and I said, Hold my hands, I don't know what's happening to me. I asked, What do you see? 'Cause she sees past lives now, and I just started sobbing. You know when I sob, I sob.

Then all of a sudden I was reliving the crucifixion of Peter. So, I must have really been Peter. I never really believed that. I have never really forgiven my past life as Peter, deserting the Christ, and they crucified me upside down, and I felt all the blood coming to my head.

I hadn't said anything about what I was experiencing, and

this bird said, "I see a man, like a Roman Soldier. He had a rope around your right shoulder, and your neck, so he wouldn't break your neck, and dragging you towards the cross that they crucified you on."

I was trying to stand up and not crawl. It was horrible, absolutely horrible. And I felt so unworthy. and degraded. It was horrible! Anyway, strange how the pressure went off my neck, and the pain is really better today. I feel new life coming into me. As we relived the silly thing, this bird kept trying to get me to say, 'You are Peter.' I wouldn't accept I was Peter because of the unworthiness of it. So, I asked God to help me forgive that lifetime, if I was Peter (ha, ha), which ain't no big thing.

And then she described what Peter looked like. He's a stocky, short man with a lot of unruly hair, a very rough, fisherman. Very stubborn. Kinda reddish brown hair and blue eyes. It was fascinating. Any hoo. It was quite an experience.

Then I came in here and my eyes went haywire. I couldn't really see very good. Went to sleep. When I woke up, some of the pain, some of the pressure was released. So, whatever. You know, you believe all things and hope all things, and try to endure all things. Anyway, this morning I feel new life coming into my bones. I feel a joy of living today.

***

Here I am sitting in the Avalon Hotel in Virginia Beach, Virginia. Only God knows the flight of a little bird! And Baby it's cold outside! Cherie and I left Long Beach a week ago and by the grace of God, made it after a blow-out in El Paso, a chewed up fan belt and the alternator froze in Brunswick, Georgia. We cut the belt and rode in on the battery plus a wing and a prayer. Arrived here with $11.00, and Little Boss said a room on the ocean could be had for $10. Lo and behold, after looking all over, found this one!

The birds in Hawaii wired us some green energy and we paid a week's rent (only $26 for two which is a human miracle in Virginia Beach)! God does take care of his birds and all others too, only they don't know it is God. Funzee.

Went to an AA meeting. Met a commander in the Navy in

Norfolk. Lots of action going on in the drug centers and alcohol centers here. Good meetings. A navy bird took the alternator last night to see if he can salvage it. Cherie is looking for work, and more will be revealed. Love and Service is our life and reckon God has some work for us here. Make love not war.

My bones miss Hawaii, but a bird of mine in California gave me a big sheep lined coat, and it saved me life.

Larry, you're not too far from us in Georgia. Put on your silver wings and fly over. It is a white world. But the sun does shine through!

3

MEETING FLOBIRD

God is my employer, and He doesn't pay my wages much in green energy. He pays my wages in sick little birds with broken wings.

-- Flobird

CHERIE

Most of the time Flobird was totally content, in bliss consciousness as she called it. But periodically she would become frustrated towards people not getting it and at life in general, and she would cry, cuss God, and scream that she just wanted to die. But she always snapped out of it. She had a faith in God and life that was unshakable 99% of the time. I had that kind of faith in her.

I experienced many faces of Flobird in her lifetime. When I was a child, she was my protector. As I reached my teens, she became my competitor. As a young adult, she was my teacher. Things that stand out most in my memory: She liked to dress the girls in the family (my sister Marchand, me, and her) in the same outfits; we always had new Easter outfits, new dolls for Christmas; she tried to buy us everything we wanted even if she had to go into debt for it; she didn't like to cook; she read voraciously; she drank a lot of alcohol, and she loved the sun. Frequently, when I'd come home from school, I would find her sitting on the patio enjoying the afternoon sun with a drink in one hand and her ever-burning cigarette in the other.

When I was fourteen she got sober...and divorced, in that order. After the divorce, I continued to live with her, and Marchand went to live with dad.

Sobriety and sharing that sobriety with others became the most important thing in her life. I often went with her when she'd go and talk to someone who wanted to get sober. And when I'd have a party, my friends would end up in her room listening as she shared her experience, strength and hope. I felt threatened because of this and began feeling as if I needed to compete with her for their attention. But the competition was only in my mind.

She was always bringing people home to help them sober up. One time she brought this man home that had been in Patten State Hospital. He was diagnosed as having a wet brain, meaning that alcohol had destroyed some of his brain cells, and he wasn't able to function in society. This was in the early '60's. At first, he would sit in front of the TV watching programs and smoking four packs of cigarettes every day. Little by little he became capable of doing odd jobs around the house. Flobird would take him to the local AA club house, and he began helping out by serving coffee and keeping the place clean. The last time I saw him, he was managing the coffee bar at the club house.

It took me many years to realize that I let Flobird be in charge of my love life. Every time a man would enter my life that was very important to me, she would find reasons why we shouldn't be together. Sometimes it took her a few months, sometimes only days, but there was ALWAYS a reason. She packed many a bag and set them outside, asking them to leave. What amazes me as I write this, is that I was actually unaware of what was happening. I guess I thought Flobird knew best. Finally, at the age of 28, I stood up to her and said no. He was not leaving. There was no reason. We could work this out. Of course, the relationship ended eventually, but not for a couple of years.

Flobird had a great influence on many areas of my life, and my sister's life.

MARCHAND

Flobird was my mother, sponsor, friend. When I think of her I have flashes of tricycles, falling down and her kissing my scrapes, cutting my bangs. She never thought she was a good mother. She tried to live her desires for dolls by giving Sis and I one every year for Christmas. All I wanted was horses and stuffed animals.

I remember looking at her when I was a child and thinking she was ugly. I don't know if I got that from my own concept or listening to her say she was ugly. I remember this one time when she played golf and her hair was real short. I looked at her and thought how beautiful she was. But there were other times when I was ashamed to be with her.

And I felt guilty. I could never understand what that was. My first husband was always ashamed to walk down the street with her and me. One time in Germany we were all walking down the street, and I realized he had backed up about four paces.

I could be in pain, feel like I was dying, and go in and be by her side. She'd put her arms around me, and I'd cry and feel like everything was going to be okay. That protective, all inclusive love that she gave continuously. I've never felt it again...until I came back into AA. There has never been anyone since her that does that, and today, I trust God, and He gives that to me.

When she and dad first separated and she was newly sober, I would sit on her bed for hours, and she would read to me from the Big Book, the Bible, and Science of Mind. We put $600 of Monopoly money in the Bible for my horse. That was one of the things that made me consciously begin to trust and believe in all things hoped for, evidence of things not seen.

I just knew that life was more than it seemed and love was the answer. Mom taught us the Golden Rule (do unto others as you would have them do unto you) even through her drinking.

I didn't know a lot of stuff about life, and I was in constant pain about life that I didn't even know I was in. But SHE knew. She knew each one of us. She knew our hearts. She knew where we were going. And all she could do was love us and let us do what we needed to do.

Flobird always seemed to arrive in people's lives at exactly the right moment as if she was summoned, especially when they had a major decision to make, or just needed some kind of spiritual guidance.

TOM TOM

In 1967-68 I lived out in Sunset Beach on the North Shore of Oahu at Combs Court. I was using drugs (but only for spiritual reasons) at that point in time. I wasn't shooting any dope. I lived next door to this empty four bedroom house. One day there was a buzz going around the neighborhood about this weird lady that had shown up. The way I remember it, Flobird came to this house next door, reached above the door, found the key, unlocked the door and walked in. A couple of days later the real estate person came to show the house, found Flobird living there, and said, "Lady, what are you doing here?"

Flobird answered, "God told me to come here."

And by what we call miracles, she lived in that house another 6 months. The rent was paid, the electricity was turned on, and it became a house for drug addicts and alcoholics to come and sober up.

She began holding a weekly meeting of Alcoholics Anonymous there. That meeting was the beginning of what was later called the Beachcombers Spiritual Progress meeting. During that first meeting I walked back and forth looking in the window checking things out. I had been taking LSD and reading different Eastern spiritual books about love and light, and all of a sudden here was this woman who radiated the stuff I had been reading. Everyone I was hanging around was trying to be on this spiritual path also, so I went and told them about her. They came and moved right in with her. That's how she entered my life and how I found Alcoholics Anonymous.

WAYNE

It began 1966, 1967 on a night I had taken a heavy overdose of barbiturates. I knew I was going to die. I could feel myself starting to leave my body and being totally terrified. I was thinking, this is it. I'm dying. I can remember praying to God saying, "God, please help me," before passing out. When I woke up Tom was banging on my door and saying, "Hey Wayne, we're using too many drugs. Let's move to Hawaii."

And we did. We got to Hawaii, found a house to rent on the beach on the North Shore on the island of Oahu. We were back three or four houses from what became known as the God House. Shortly after we moved in, I was talking to a guy who lived close by, and Flobird was walking toward us. He said, "Look out for her. She's nuts. Stay away from her. She's nothing but trouble."

Of course that piqued my interest right away. She came

walking across the parking lot, and across the driveway right toward us. She was wearing a bikini, and she had long, long hair. She was holding a cigarette. As she walked up to me, she stuck out her hand and said, "Hi. My name is Flobird. I'm a happy, grateful alcoholic." I couldn't believe what I was hearing. She continued with, "I'm having a meeting at my house tonight. Why don't you come."

I went home and told Tom we had a real nut case living next door to us. But we started talking to her, and we started going to the meetings.

ANNE

I was 33 years old with three teenage children. I was into my fourth marriage and had served time in jail for writing hot checks while under the influence of alcohol. I hated myself and thought everyone else hated me also. Even God.

An AA friend took me to Huntington Beach to see Flobird hoping that maybe she could help me. I had been going to AA meetings for about a year but could not stay sober.

The minute Flobird looked at me, I could see in her eyes and big smile that she loved and accepted me just as I was, a full-blown alcoholic dying on the vine. I felt I was a hopeless case, but Flobird taught me to see I was worthy of sobriety and a full happy life. She welcomed me back into her world of love and sobriety each time I had a relapse. She never gave up on me even when everyone else in AA had. She just kept telling me how beautiful and wonderful I was. I finally believed her. From 1965 to 1969 Flobird sponsored and worked with me. I had my last drink July 8, 1969. I have been sober and clean since then. Thank you, my dear Flobird.

KAYE

I met Flobird in 1963 when I was 14 years old. She planted a seed in me that continues to grow today. She gave me a security I desperately needed in my life.

Flobird: A Bird's Eye View

CLAY

When I stop and think about Flobird...do you realize that was over 30 years ago? I remember when I was 18, and I believe Cherie was 13, and I was beginning to date her. Her father was so mad, he wanted to kill me, but Flobird was very calm and cool. All she said was, "Are you doing anything wrong?" Well, we weren't, and that was good enough for her.

She had the ability to place trust in people. You had no reason to lie to her for she could look at you and know the truth. I remember the slumber parties Cherie would have, and she would walk in, never turn on the lights, and say, "I hope there are no boys in the house." She knew we were there all the time.

She was like my mother. They seemed to be different than most parents at that time who were tired of their kids by the time we were teenagers.

When I was around Flobird in her house, I felt like I was home. She talked to me like I was part of her. She trusted me like I was part of her. I raised my kids that way. I have all girls, and they have a lot of friends who call me Dad.

Bottom line is that I liked my mother's attitude and Flobird's for the respect they had for us as people. They wanted respect, and they gave us the same as we were growing up. And we would do dumb things, but they were always there for us as long as we needed them.

TOM

She appeared to be a very homely looking person at first. Basically unattractive. And then, within moments of being with her, it was obvious how beautiful she was. It was that beauty, too, that I don't think I ever experienced in my life. I was 21 years old when I met her, and I hadn't had a whole lot of life experience, but it was the first time that I knew what real inner beauty was, and how inner beauty really dominates outer appearance.

I've since realized over the years with myself and other

people that when you are at one with God and you are attuned to the love of the universe you glow, you just glow. Just like how a pregnant woman looks so beautiful too. They are in tune with the creative force.

She had amazing stamina and amazing endurance physically and emotionally. Just unbelievable. Most of the people that were with her when I met her were very, very young, and on an energy level, she would run circles around us. She'd keep going and going and going. She was like that Ever Ready battery. It keeps going, and going, and going. And the energy always came from love. I remember I used to feel so puny because I was on my way down, I was tired, I just wanted to check out for the day - which is okay - which is human. But I was living with someone like her who was on call 24 hours a day, and not because she had to be (although I believe she had to be), but because she wanted to be as well. And she would say, "Humility is knowing that you are 100% powerless over life and everything in it, and being happy about it." She lived it. She really, really lived it.

First time I actually talked to Flobird, I was resistant towards it. I watched others go into her room to talk to her, but I rebelled against it. My ego rebelled against it. I was in a lot of inner struggle. I was only clean a matter of days, and there were questions I had. There was this God thing. I had no belief in God, no concept of God. I had my old Catholic concept which I didn't even know I had. So I went into her room, and she was sitting there on her bed with her Love That Red lipstick on, her hair up in a bun, her books laying all around her, and she was wearing some kind of a white gown, her pillows all propped up. She held her burning cigarette, and she had this big smile on her face that seemed to take up the whole bottom of her face.

"Hi Bird. How ya' doin' sweetheart. Come on in. Sit down."

I was in my Bob Dillon serious look, and I sat down, took a breath and said, "Okay. This God thing. If there's a God, this God has to have a plan for me. Right?"

She goes, "Right."

"In other words, you have to have a will."

She says, "Right."

"So, okay, what is God's will for me?"

And she said, "Sweetheart, God's will for you is to live, love, laugh and be happy for His sake. Because you're an expression of God. God can only live through you. Without you God has no expression. You're His unique expression. An expression that He has created and chosen for Himself.

"When you're locked in your selfishness and you're locked in your anger, your fear, your greed, and your shame, you block the presence of God. You block the expression of God in your life. God can't be the Tom that He created. He can't express Himself to His full potential. That's what the 12 Steps are all about. Uncovering, discovering, and opening up that channel, which is the purpose for all of this, to open up the channel so God can express himself. So God can be free in you. Because God in you as you is you. But you should never forget that God is greater than you."

That kicked off my concept of God. If I'm supposed to find a God like it said in the Big Book, a God that makes sense to me, a God that is loving, then this would be the God. A God that would want these things for me - to live, love, laugh and be happy for His sake. Always the simplicity of what she would say was so mind boggling. It was so simple. Always so simple.

In those early years watching her in action was something else. The example that she set for me to this day is the only example in my life that I have. I've looked around and seen lots of things going on in this world, and she set almost all the examples of the spiritual life of what I would like to aspire to. Her dedication, her absolute persistence in prayer and meditation.

I tell you, I've been in relationship after relationship, and it's a struggle all the time to get the person I'm with to understand how important it is that when I get up, I've got to get quiet. I've got to get one with God. They don't get it. First I have to have my own sanctuary, my own special place to pray and meditate. That's my stuff. I remember Flobird saying, "If you have to mediate on a toilet seat, you do it. You go to any lengths to find a mediation place."

4

HOW FLOBIRD AFFECTED LIVES

Recognize when you meet somebody else, that they're a human being too. And they have the same emotions, the same hurts, and the same problems that we all have.

-- Flobird

CHERIE

The way I live my life today is directly related to what Flobird taught. Her ideas of the AA program, her ideas of life, death, birth, abundance, God...so many things. I'd have to say that every area of my life has changed because of her. In the area of relationships, I learned how to be rigorously honest directly because of her. In the area of money, I know that God is my source directly because of my experience of traveling with her. In the area of work, I know that God is my employer because she pointed it out to me in the Big Book, and she lived it. She went before me as an able example. In the area of play, I learned to be as a child and see life as an adventure because she did that. She was ageless. Today, I FEEL ageless. The area of God - well, she certainly showed me that God was not somewhere out there, but was in me. She was definitely a spiritual teacher, and continues to be so today. My sister had a different experience with her than I did. She is 3 1/2 years my junior.

MARCHAND

My whole life was affected by what Flobird did and how she lived. When I was younger, she would cheer me on at swim meets believing in me and helping me believe in myself. She helped me learn to pick myself up and try again no matter how many times I would fall. She showed me a gentleness toward all and taught me there was a goodness, part of God, in all of us, and not to look at others faults, colors or inabilities, but to see only the good. I had no sense of judgment from her of the negative things about people. My life, my thinking and actions were geared to this way. Thus I never would believe that people would hurt me. Things were always my fault; the pain in my world of denial as I call it today. When I see only the good, I bypass the full picture and only experience part of life.

She taught me to do unto others as I would have them do unto me. Trusting people. Being true to one's self. To not be afraid. Doing the thing I feared to do and trusting a loving God.

Flobird: A Bird's Eye View

To love God and put others first. Always holding out a helping hand. Telling the truth was always better than any small lie, no matter how much it hurt. Honesty eliminated fear.

I remember most her warm hugs of assurance, that no matter what, things would be all right. She radiated love. I loved to watch her dance - her long rubber legs. She'd leave us notes when we got home from school.

She was radiant with love, funny, welcoming, comfortable, free to be whoever she was and say whatever she felt.

Flobird affected not only me and my sister, but she touched many, many lives. The changes that came about because of her presence, and the influence she had in some of the lives she touched could be dramatic. Some hated her, most loved her, some thought she was crazy, but all respected who she had become.

TOM TOM

I owe so much to Flobird. My whole life was changed through her influence. I'm not using today, and I haven't since meeting her. I owe it all to her. She's the one who introduced me to the 12 Steps of recovery. In those days we didn't have halfway houses and treatment centers. Being with her, traveling with her, living with her, that was my treatment center, my recovery house. That was the way I was taken out of the world as a newcomer and sheltered. It was a hard core shelter though, because you didn't get away with anything. Today they go into treatment centers for 3-6 months.

I remember her as being weather beaten. She looked like she had really lived life. She was totally detached from the physical and didn't really care about that stuff much. But she had total love and acceptance, and I was comfortable when I was with her.

I learned so much from Flobird. I'm here to try to learn to love unconditionally. To bring others into my life a little more. I watched her on the go 24 hours a day sometimes, when necessary, and sharing with other people. She dedicated her whole life to us. We wore her out.

Then there were all the other people that gathered around her. I feel that the reason I have everything I have today is because I put my spiritual program before everything else. I never desired to have 12 employees and make $100,000 a year. That was not my desire. I was on food stamps, and I was quite content. But because I put all this other stuff first, working my steps, working with others, going to meetings, practicing my Eleventh Step first, this is what has happened as a result of that. I still put most of my energy into the program. I have everything I have today because of that influence.

I did look at her as a Guru. I was her disciple. I was dedicated to her. I was always really proud to walk in the room with her. I'd get her coffee. I'd make her vegetarian sandwiches. She always called the alfalfa sprouts grass. "Oh, you made me another sandwich with grass in it?" I liked taking care of her. I was never ashamed to be seen with her. We were both kinda weird looking. I had a beard down to my waist sometimes. I remember having that real special dedication with her. And a lot of rebellion sometimes, too. I screamed at her sometimes.

HAROLD

Flobird was a lady whose goal, values and vision were beyond the world of illusion we live in. She was one of the people who came into my life by Divine Appointment at just the time I needed her inspiration, spiritual wisdom and example in my program of recovery.

KAYE

Flobird taught me many, many things. She taught me about love without a price tag. She taught me that I could seek out and rely on the power of God within me. This was a security I'd never had before.

She was tall and gangly and very tan. She had a beautiful smile and the warmest brown eyes that radiated the powerful love inside her. That powerful love and faith are what kept her frail body operating.

Flobird: A Bird's Eye View

The thing I like most about Flobird is that she made me feel good about who I was when I was around her. She accepted people and saw them through the eyes of love.

WAYNE

She was a manifestation of the Higher Power, I guess. The way she used to just be. The presence about her. The bikinis, the long hair, the contemplation. People see pictures of her, and they say, "Who is this women?" To me, she's the most beautiful, spiritual person I've ever seen. It was like looking at the Christ of God. She used to teach me to look at people and look at the Christ of God within, and not look at the outer, and sometimes I can do that with people. But it was very, very easy for her. I just looked at Flobird and knew she was an expression of a Higher Power. She didn't have great outer beauty, but she had that inner beauty which just shown. I'd look at her, and look at her eyes, and her sparkle, the twinkle in her eye, and her enjoyment of life. She taught me to live, love, laugh and be happy. That's what she told me this life was about. "Learn how to do it, Wayne." And this is what I've tried to do.

My whole life changed when she entered it. At that point in my life, I was totally adrift. Didn't know where to go, what to do, or who I was. All I knew was to take drugs to stop hurting.

I got off on this thing about her alcoholism, because I didn't do alcohol. Being better than. But I used to sit and listen to her for hours, then go around and listen to her work with other alcoholics. In the insanity of my program, I used to sell drugs to the people she was trying to help. But I used to listen to her, and she struck a cord inside of me. Something turned that light on inside of me that I was searching for. We had taken a lot of acid, and there was always that glimpse of something JUST beyond...if I took just a little bit more, I could just go a little bit farther, then I would reach it.

And all of a sudden, here's Flobird sitting in what she called the God House, and the whole situation is so bizarre, I can't believe it. She's living free, the Landlord let her move in. I didn't know what that whole thing was about. Scary, and everything else, but I listened to her, and there was this thing coming off her - this radiance. And I remember one time sitting and looking at her on the couch and seeing just a total glow around her, and thinking, My god, am I having a flashback or what. It was a feeling that was inside there. That tremendous peace or love that she had and transferred to those around her. She changed my whole life from that point on.

As far as I'm concerned, my whole life was not lived until I met Flobird. From that point on I started living life. Doing everything that she said. Everything she did. I spent a lot of years following her around. Everything I am today is because of what the Higher Power through her told me, and she was a direct channel. I believe that. Everything that she would say, and she would write in her journals just came true. It was an incredible living experience being around her.

With the outpouring of love and understanding, I watched her very carefully. I'm very reserved. I really watch people. I'm on guard. And there are so many cons and everything going around, so I reserve judgment. I sat back and watched her, and it amazed me how she worked with people. She worked with Mike different than she worked with Jim, and she worked with Jim different than she worked with Jane, and Doug, and the way that she worked in my life was totally different. She was always gentle. We had our ups and downs at times, but she never attacked me per se like she did some of the others. She handled me way differently than she did everybody else, and yet it was the exact way I needed to be handled. She gave me the love I needed to feel at that point in time. I'm sure if she'd attacked me like she did some of the others, I'd have split. I couldn't have taken it at that point in my life.

Basically she's changed my whole life. My whole life is based on the principles she taught me which are the principles of the program, but they came from a different side. Flobird had many, many sides to her. I watched a lot of them, and they were all different, when she worked with people. In my case she was very gentle, very loving all the time.

The thing I liked least about her was her smoking, and the way she seemed to protect Marchand. I traveled with her and with Marchand, and it became a tough thing. She protected Marchand like crazy. These are my honest feelings. I know there were a lot of things that I understand today but didn't then. Things like, it was because she was her daughter, that she always protected Marchand, looked after Marchand, held Marchand's hand. And I think there were times that I felt that she could have let Marchand take some of her knocks on her own. Anyway, that used to cause a bit of a rift.

ANNE

Flobird was God made manifest, and my whole life was changed because of Flobird's love and understanding of a dying alcoholic.

MIKE

Flo was the most spiritual person that I have ever met in this life. A beautiful soul and spirit. I remember Flobird being tall and lanky, with very long brown/gray hair, her skin was deep brown from loving and living in the sun. She was always smoking a cigarette, and her eyes shone with love. She was one of the happiest people that I have ever known; she loved people and was constantly with people.

Flobird also loved to spend time alone with God, and she was forever reading metaphysical and spiritual books. Many quiet times for reading, and writing in her spiritual journal or meditating.

A great deal of my AA program and thinking is a direct result of my months and years of living with Flobird or being with her. Flobird is and has been the most important spiritual influence in my life. I saw her through my eyes and heard her through my ears, and I think of her always as my spiritual teacher in human form. She was always my friend and was always there for me. I loved her in a very special way.

I loved her and could only see her love of life and humanity. Flobird did have feet of clay and was very human, but my love for her, and what I saw with my own eyes overshadowed any shortcomings and character defects that she may have had. Flobird was NOT my Higher Power. She was human, and I took her off the pedestal after my first year with her.

GOLDENEAGLE

Flobird was a beach-combing Mother Teresa of the cast out and hopeless addicts and alcoholics and lost youth of her day. The ugliest, skinniest women I ever knew. Also the most beautiful, radiant and loving one.

How do I begin to tell you about all the changes in my life? I was 17 when I met her. Fearful, unsure, lost, afraid of everything and everyone. Flobird immediately within minutes of meeting her, asked me if I was a homosexual. I do not remember what I said, except that she had me doing an inventory of my life and contemplating it before I left. Eventually I completed several sexual ones.

At her urging 18 months later, January 1974, I had my first adult male sexual experience. She helped me see that God loved me and everyone; it didn't matter what we did in bed. God loved us unconditionally, and if we loved one another unconditionally, there was no sin! So, I became a sexual being as a result of Flobird. Came out!

She also in later years was to tell me that sex would become an addiction and compulsion for me, and that I would recover by using the 12 Steps. How true! In July of 1984 I went to Sex & Love Addicts Anonymous and have been sexually sober, abstinent from addictive and compulsive sex since then.

My concepts, faith and beliefs in God changed as a result of her being in my life. To this day I trust God when all else fails. Often first before even taking action.

My descent into the abyss of active alcoholism addiction was averted because of Flobird's insistence I work the 12 Steps of the Alcoholics Anonymous program as best I could in all my affairs. I am most certain today that had I not found the 12 Steps, Flobird's teaching of them, spirituality and God, my life would have been much different. If I had survived, remained alive, for long. I do not believe I would have.

I considered myself a potential alcoholic until December 1975, had my last drink on New Year's Eve 1975. A healthy fear of alcohol has ensued since then. So I embarked on a life practicing the 12 Steps and got rudimentary basic spiritual lessons and tools, and in many ways began the process of being set free from my past in this body, and karma from previous lives. And the process continues today.

Flobird could be very frustrating about making any decision(s) and at times self-righteous and indignant and intolerant of other's struggles with spiritual principles and life's difficulties and/or their unwillingness to see things as simply black and white as she did (in her way of understanding).

TOM

Once I was part of Flobird's life force or flock and was in her world, it was pretty amazing what happened. I became extremely obedient towards her. A lot of people cringe at that thought because of the occult type things, but I don't think people understand what that is. It's sort of a discipleship. It really is a student/teacher relationship.

Flobird had power over me. There is no doubt about it. And I don't mean power in the negative sense. Flobird took one look at me, and my whole disposition changed. I would fight and rebel against it, but I was willing to learn from this very gifted person. Willing to learn how to live, love, laugh and be happy. In that respect, I had to learn to follow at times regardless of whatever will - whether that will came directly from God or God through Flobird, or Flobird through God, or how ever you want to put it.

A tremendous gift she gave all of us was her ability to form new terminology about life and what was going on, particularly on the spiritual path.

Nowadays if you are down and depressed, the psychologist or psychiatrist calls it depression. They have all kinds of ways of gauging what kind of depression you're in, what kind of person you are, if you're this type of personality or that type of personality. But Flobird considered any change we went through as being spiritual growth. She would describe our deep depressions as body changes and would say that our whole body was being transformed into light. She called it Baptism by fire. She never used the term depression. And we all went along with that. We called it pains of spiritual growth, dark nights of the soul. She gave meaning and purpose to what we were going through. Whereas, nowadays, if you're depressed, there's no meaning to it. You're just depressed.

She was ruthless in the way she would deal with us. So many times we would all be sitting around in a comfortable living room or maybe in a not so comfortable setting like a camp site, and we would all be bitching at each other and whining and moaning and groaning when suddenly she would walk out of wherever she was at, look at us and say, 'You selfish self-centered little piss-ants. Get off your ass and get into some love-in-action.'

She would constantly tell us to do love and service, and love-in-action was the magic way. I used to write it in my journal, "Love-in-action is the magic way. Love-in-action is the magic way. God is all there is. Which is interesting, too, because I've read tons of books and listened to tons of spiritual teachers and stuff, and she is the only one that ever said that God was all there was. Her theory was as simple as you could get it. God is all there is. God is the doer of all the actions. Although I don't apply that principal all the time in my life today, if I find myself out there, it's the simplicity that comes back to me.

The early impressions are with me to this day. She used to tell me that God loves you and I love you. Your only problem is that you have to accept it. She couldn't have been more right on.

She was way ahead of her time in dealing with depressed feelings and the anger and hate. Because of my ego and my pride, I wouldn't allow myself to express the anger and hate that was inside of me. I would suppress it even more. And from the VERY beginning she was aware of it. The reason she was aware of it was because she experienced it. She would come to me and tell me, "When are you going to get the anger

out of you? When are you going to get your hate out? When are you going to get your hate out at me?" She used to really piss me off when she'd say that. I'd tell her, "I don't want to hate you. I don't want to take my anger out on you."
And yet, it was almost like she knew she had to take on the world or person, and be a channel for God to work through her, letting others vent their rage.

It took many, many years, almost 20 years, before I got down to really expressing that rage and anger inside of me. And when it came out, it was unbelievable. So again, she was right on.
I'd been on the Mainland and wanted to come back to Hawaii. I became aware of another spiritual truth that she talked about. You lose your process of making your own decisions, of what you're going to do, where you're going to go. She said you just have to wait for guidance. You can't make decisions like that any more. You gotta follow your heart and look for God's work. And as much as I wanted to come back to Hawaii, I couldn't. I couldn't leave California. I knew I had to be right there until the time came. Then I got a letter from Flobird that said, 'Wouldn't it be magical and wonderful and mysterious if we were to meet again at Sunset Beach on December 17 for my first AA birthday'? That's when I knew; the doors opened up; the path was paved.

Flobird was really a teacher. Her goal was to become useless to us. To bring us to a point on this path where we didn't need her anymore. As a group, that's what happened. She really did bring us to a place where we all pretty much found ourselves and were firmly on the path. We didn't need Flobird to make our decisions. So she was successful.

I think and believe that God had a role for Flobird in this life. In her living that role, there were a lot of areas in life that Flobird just couldn't live. If she could have, she probably wouldn't have had the role that she did.

She was always consistent. You could rely on that. The love was consistent. The giving was consistent. The availability was consistent. More consistent than anyone else I've ever seen in my life. Her readiness to serve. Her readiness to go anywhere at any time. I think that if I had not lived with somebody like Flobird and seen her actually put it into action in the way that she did, and I'd just read about it, it would just be a theory. It would just be an interesting spiritual theory. But I watched this woman do this stuff day in and day out. It was phenomenal. It worked. What ever she did, it worked, all the time. No laws could stand in God's way. No spiritual laws, no physical laws, no man made laws. God could do anything He wanted to do. Open the doors in any way He wanted to open the doors. Flobird showed me that. I had experiences in life that told me, yes, it's there. One of her old sayings, "If you have faith and never doubt, you'll know what God is all about." That was true for me.

When we lived in New Mexico, things kind of shifted. My relationship with Flobird had changed and grown. I grew more independent, as we all did. It was empowering for us to be living in the mountains and building our own homes, having our own businesses. Gave us a strong sense of self and our ability to do things.

Living on the wing from this place to that place is a hard way to live. There's no security involved. I think New Mexico was the first time we saw some outer success and our confidence in ourselves to do things.

We began living there without Flobird. Flobird joined us later but only for brief periods. So mostly it was run by us. The Beachcombers meeting was run by us. Traditionally for years Flobird always ran every Beachcombers meeting.

I remember Cherie's writings about the Beachcombers group. Flobird always loved the group, and she always gave a little talk after everybody spoke. The meeting was always open ended and could last up to six hours. We all just sat there. It was an incredible experience for anyone who came to that group. There were only a few of us that stayed consistent with the group and actually sat in the meeting and not leave. The Beachcombers meeting was, in my opinion, a great source for group. That was where a lot of the opportunities for us to get our feelings out were presented, a place where Flobird could be totally present with anybody and put herself out there in that unique way that she had. It was one thing sitting in a room and talking to her one on one, but when she sat in a room talking to 40-50 people, sitting on the floor doing her thing, she was phenomenal. What came out of her was always phenomenal.

I really wish back then that somebody had been sitting around with tape recorders taping her dialogues. Because those were wonderful times. There were times I would be sitting there, and she would be talking, and I would be saying to myself, this is the most beautiful, loving, human person I've ever heard in my life.

It was such an inspiration to just listen to her. To watch her mannerisms, her grace. She had tremendous grace. She had charisma. When she would be talking to somebody, she wasn't performing, she wasn't just talking; it was God working through her. It was great.

But Flobird was dealing with her own inner stuff too. I remember she came over once after she'd been alone for quite awhile. She had beat herself, pinched herself all over. Everything hurt so much that she'd slapped and scratched herself, and she was crying. We were all just sitting there going, God, what can we do for her? When you beat yourself, hit yourself, your body is not a very attractive thing to show to people. But she was there. She was always there.

Many times Flobird would listen to us moan and groan, bitch and complain. She would sit patiently, absorbing our hate, and then she would retire to her room, and in silent meditation, give the hate to God. We would write letters of apology, letters of love, letters to share her birthdays.

Aloha Beautiful and divine lady,
All that is very, very beautiful and very wonderful, I wish upon thee. I love you. Thank you so much for absorbing all my selfish and self-centeredness over the past six years. Most of the time I was never aware of what it did to you. Today I am, and it hurts my heart within. Yet I am powerless when I get caught up in my own orbit and can't see out of my own learning.

To be aware of all my brothers' and sisters' sufferings and needs is the beginning. There is hope for all of us, Flobird. It has not been in vain. 'Tis different inside of this temple than it was six years ago. Thank you is all I can say, besides I love you. It's truly near the golden age of love and light. I can't deny it. I look outside at this beautiful kingdom, the Kona Coast of Hawaii, and by His grace the kingdom within is as beautiful as this pure Hawaiian day. So, let's start livin', lovin', laughin' and being happy. Gonna go give it all away just for today. May the sun, ocean, and waves, and most of all the pure love that all your birds have for you, heal you now. Be happy and blissful. God is loving us now.

Aloha Flobird,
   I just want to say I love you and am so grateful for this gift of sharing life with you. For me it's a total experience in the highest magnitude just to know you and be one bird chosen by God to be taught and trained by your able example of love without a price tag.
   I know the cup God has given you is being given to me. I'm not the best at reaching out for it. I know one day I will wear it as a crown as you do the cup of world service. But for today, thanks for loving me and showing me how neat it is. Thanks for walking with me through each of my fears and doubts, and all my puny selfishness; for watching over me as I was pruned with all your love and compassion, and for hurting with me when my soul was hurting. I could go on, and on, and on. And in my heart I do.
   There's one thing happening in our group that is fantastic. Almost like we're coming of age, because I've never felt such a oneness and joy and togetherness as I do today. Maybe it's always been there, and I just haven't been aware of it. The love and oneness I feel towards everyone is something else. A complete thrusting forward movement all clothed in love, gratitude, service, and unity. It's almost so neat that I am afraid to breathe for fear of bursting into a billion lights of something that goes beyond joy. I know God is happy. Something like the joy He felt that day at the Jordan when John baptized Jesus and

Flobird: A Bird's Eye View

the dove descended, and God said, "This is my son with whom I am well pleased", and then loosed him on the world to scatter love and all the keys of His kingdom.

Guess I'm still going through the crucifixion part. Where my little ego is on the cross, dying. Soon some clown will come along and crown me King of the Jews, and it will be done, and a new bird will come popping out of a tomb and giggling will say, "And you, too, can be a bird." Funzee. Loving you with wings.

Good morning mother who is not my mother,

I wanted to say how grateful I am I came through you and how grateful I am that I was led to AA through you. Fourteen years ago today, a whole new life opened up. Wow! So many changes inner and outer and each one so necessary. You've been that special link to connect me to God whenever I felt doubt. By your faith I've been healed many times over. You're my able example of life abundantly. You've gone before us as Jesus did to lay the path and light the way, and when we stumble and feel we're falling, you're always there to help. You do patch our broken wings and teach us to fly all over again. The things we know deep inside, you help us uncover and see for ourselves. You are a shining light for all who wish to see. How grateful I am to thee. Someday I hope I can be as you are, and give the selfless love you give to all. You are my able example. Thank you for going before me to light my way.

November, 1976
Aloha Joy bird of my life,

Wishing you a beautiful love birthday. Thank you for your love and help in my times of change and growth.

September 9, 1976
Has anybody thanked you
for being you today?
Or said how much they loved you,
or asked you out to play?

You do so many little things
around this home of ours.
Does anyone ever stop and say,
"Hey, thank you for your hours!"
Thanks for washing all the clothes;
thanks for cleaning house;
the way you move so quickly here,
you must be some part mouse.
Thanks for keeping everything
so nice and sparkly clean.
Thanks so much for being you,
and loving all that's seen.

Happy Birthday beautiful one. So happy to be near you and one of you. You bring me love, hope and show me all the beauty in life and God. Thank you for the strength you give - your love.

November 1, 1975

Fifteen years ago, one day at a time you walked through the doors of AA. You had nothing to lose. You'd lost it all; you were shown a new way. You cried out for help and people were there holding their hands out to you. They said, "Follow me down the road to this life filled with things old but brand new."

You went willingly. You did not ask why. You just did all that they said. You found you were breathing, you found you could smile, You'd found your way back from the dead. And so you went off to give it away and try loving people right now. No matter what, you kept trying to give, and teaching to others the H.O.W.

By taking the 1st Step and on through the 12, by walking the pathway to start, you've shown to us all the right way to go if we want a love-filled heart.

Aloha Flobird,

Well, here we go again. The cycle of time repeats itself. Our desires repeat themselves. But thank God, God never repeats Himself. And so a new adventure. One thing for sure, spiritual progress is always constant whether the body is in motion or sitting still.

I've been watching you this past week and can tell the body has been so weary. I've really been feeling a sadness. I guess it's times like this when I see you quietly hanging in there that I want to be with you and stand by you. God just keeps sending you the so called hopeless ones no matter what condition you are in. And it never ceases to amaze me to see you responding in the way you do. The choicelessness just gives all the more glory to God.

It's what you are that I want to be. And I guess that's for God's sake alone as there isn't anything in it for the self. There is no escaping our destiny to be service fools and clowns. Bill Wilson was one. Anonymous unto himself. Endowed with the rarest kind of humility. I get the feeling Jesus on the cross didn't know what He was doing either. And yet in that place beyond thought, we have all-knowing, and in there, all men are one.

Hope the ol' bod' perks up and new energy pours in. Thanks for your life. I do salute you!

5

LIKES AND DISLIKES

If you haven't tried shootin' up in your hands, use your hands, or use your toes. Get it out of your system. Hit bottom - if you still want to die. If you want to live, I'll go to any length to help you.

-- Flobird

CHERIE

Though overall Flobird was loved, there were many things people didn't like about her. From my perspective she had a built-in denial system regarding some areas of her life. When Flobird would react to me, I'd say it was because she hadn't forgiven her big sister (my personality is very much like hers was), But she would deny it.

She had rationalizations for her continuing to smoke (she burned tobacco fields in a past life, so she was making up for it in this one. Or, it kept her human. If she gave up smoking then she'd float away).

There were many, many things about herself that Flobird refused to deal with. Her sisters for one. Before she died, Marchand called her older sister, Lorraine, and I called her younger sister, Vivian, to let them know what was happening. Flobird was very angry with both of us, as she didn't want to contact either of them.

I wasn't the only one who could see her humanity through her spirituality. But it didn't make us love her any less.

MARCHAND

The thing I liked least about her was that she felt she had to protect me from men or people she was afraid would hurt me. It seemed more detrimental for me in later years. She knew how vulnerable and innocent our hearts were, that there was a lot of pain in the world. She had been there and done that, and loved me.

Toward the end I think she knew there wasn't anything she could to do keep me from the pains of life. I don't know that that is what I really liked least about her, but I do know she protected me because she loved me so much. Possibly she felt she could keep me from living the pains of life as she had. I believe the pain in her heart was possibly too much for her to bear as a mother, so in reality, she was protecting herself through me and other birds. I just thought she was right and didn't really know she was protecting me.

TOM TOM

I thought there were some wicked people on this Earth because that's how Flobird depicted them. But, you will find that any holy person still has work to do. She had a lot of character defects, faults, and the way she saw things. The funny thing about this smoking thing, I wouldn't give her a cigarette today. I'd slap her silly. I wouldn't be able to be around them and have her smoke in my house.

ELISA

I would describe her as personality disordered who had a massive spiritual experience and spent the rest of her life living that experience. The thing I like least about her was her absolutism.

KAYE

The thing I liked least about Flobird was that you couldn't hide your true self from her.

WAYNE

The thing I liked least about her was her smoking, and the way she seemed to protect Marchand. I traveled with her and with Marchand, and it became a tough thing. She protected Marchand like crazy. That is just my honest feelings. I know there were a lot of things that I understand today, because she was her daughter, and whatever, but she always protected Marchand, looked after Marchand, held Marchand's hand. And I think there were times that I felt that she could have let Marchand take some of her knocks on her own. Anyway, that used to cause a bit of a rift.

GOLDENEAGLE

She could be very frustrating about making any decision(s), and at times self-righteous, indignant, and intolerant of other's struggles with spiritual principles and life's difficulties and/or their unwillingness to see things as simply black and white as she did in her way.

MIKE

I loved her and could only see her love of life and humanity. Flobird did have feet of clay and was very human, but my love for her and what I saw with my own eyes overshadowed any shortcomings and character defects that she may have had because of my love for her and what she represented. Flobird was NOT my Higher Power. She was human, not on a pedestal after my first year with her.

TOM

There were a lot of things about Flobird I didn't like. I didn't think she was great with relationships. This was an area of Flobird's life she never resolved - her own childhood. She had all this wonderful, beautiful, connectedness, but she was also a human being and had a ton of unresolved stuff in her life.

Her rationalizing about cigarette smoking, 'It's not me that smokes. It's the cigarette that smokes. It keeps my feet on the ground.' The bottom line was that she was hooked. Big Time. Granted, Flobird was powerless and couldn't stop smoking. That part was obvious. Yet for someone who was so keenly aware of addiction as she was and worked with people on that level, she could not see her own stuff.

Another thing I didn't like about her was her almost narcissus relationship with Marchand, and it was something that all of us could see. We'd confront her on it, but she would deny it absolutely. She had a thing with Marchand where she wouldn't let Marchand have her own life. In my opinion, Flobird couldn't accept she was just Marchand's mother. And she would even deny she was acting like a mother. She'd argue that we're all just alcoholics and drug addicts like everyone else. Well, that wasn't true with Marchand, and she would jump right into Marchand's life, and try to control it, especially where men were concerned.

She was not one you could come up against and argue with. Arguing with Flobird just didn't work. I can't remember seeing her getting into something with someone and her saying, "Gee, you're right." She came from a certain premise, and that's where she stayed.

Actually, Cherie was the only one that I know of that would go toe to toe with Flobird. She didn't seem to be afraid of her in that way. A lot of times when we'd all get together and decide that something needed to be said, we'd all go, "Yeah, Cherie, you go tell her." We were all like little kids staying in the background saying, "Cherie's going to confront her."

Flobird was very strong at holding her ground. I'd watch Cherie get into it with her, and go away crying because Flobird wouldn't give up or give in to Cherie's feelings and opinions. That was a character flaw of Flobird's.

6

TRAVELING WITH FLOBIRD

I woke up one morning near the end of 1970, and in my meditation I got, "Go to Egypt by boat." I told the group that was with me, "I gotta go to Egypt. Anybody want to go with me?" I had four volunteers.

-- Flobird

CHERIE

When Flobird got a feeling to go some place, she never questioned the how or the why. She just became ready to go and listened for that still small voice of her "Little Boss" to tell her the next indicated step.

I lived and traveled with her from 1961 through 1977. As I explained earlier, the first trip I made with her sober was in 1961 to Imperial Beach, California where she lived for 40 days. I spent a few days at the beginning of those 40 days, and a week at the end. The thing I remember most about that time was how the fishermen in the area would bring her fresh fish they had caught to eat. And the Hell's Angels, a motorcycle gang of those days, would stop by and bring her cigarettes and food. She was like a magnet. She drew people to her wherever she was. Even in the middle of nowhere.

I moved to Hawaii in 1970 and spent seven months living in tents in the parks on the Big Island of Hawaii with Flobird and several other people. We moved every two weeks because of the time limits imposed by Parks and Recreation. There were ten of us, including kids, living in three tents.

It seemed that everyone on the island including the police knew Flobird. If the police found an alcoholic or drug addict that needed help, they would bring them to her at whatever park we were staying. She even received mail addressed simply, "Flobird, Spencer Park, Hawaii."

She was absolutely fearless. One night we were camped at Whittington Park near the town of Naalehu. Hawaiians came to this park frequently to camp and fish. In the '70's when a Hawaiian had drunk a lot of Primo, which was the name of the local beer, they would get rather violent, so they were called Primo Warriors.

This one particular night there were a couple of warriors in the park getting rather loud and obnoxious. Flobird came out of her tent holding this long stick which looked like a cane, stood with her feet spread slightly apart, the cane-stick poised at her side on the ground, her left eyebrow raised. She was wearing a long white nightgown, and her waist-length hair was loose and hanging down her back, gently moving in the breeze. She looked at these two Primo Warriors and said in her most authoritative voice, "What are you doing?!"

Now, that in itself doesn't seem like much, but in Hawaii, there is a belief in a lady called Madam Pele who is the Volcano Goddess, and people who have sworn they have seen her, say she looks just about the way Flobird looked that night. These Primo Warriors backed away, apologizing for disturbing her and took off without a second glance.

Every day was an adventure with Flobird. You never knew what was around the next corner. In April of 1971 while we were camped in Lapahoehoe Park, she came out of her tent one morning and announced, "Little Boss told me to go to Egypt by boat. Anyone want to come?" Well, I and three others figured we weren't doing anything else, so we decided to join her.

The first leg of our journey was to the island of Oahu where we regrouped and made plans. We each set off in different directions to do what we needed to do, and finally met in Venice, California where we bought a car and drove from California to Virginia Beach, Virginia.

The trip across country was, as always, an adventure in itself. One particular incident stands out in my memory. We were very close to the border of Virginia, and the car developed this weird knocking noise. We, of course, had very little money, certainly not enough to spend on the car. So Flobird said we could spiritualize the car. All we needed to do was pray for it. We did. And by the time we crossed the border into Virginia, the car quit making the noise.

We moved into a hotel, put our pictures on the walls, and our clothes in the drawers and closets just as if we planned to be there for a long time. Flobird said when you live in the now, a day is an eternity, and home is where the heart is. So, everywhere we landed was home for as long as we were there.

I got a job the next day working at Hardy's. One week later, she got a prepare to leave this place. The next day we packed up and headed for Miami Beach, Florida. We stayed there long enough to get our passports in order and meet some people, one of whom went with us to Germany.

In Germany we visited with one of the birds who was stationed there and needed help to stay sober. We bought a van, drove through Italy, Spain, and across the top of Africa. We had to sell clothes and anything we could find in order to eat. We ate a lot of cheese. One of our members was a natural salesman and a compulsive eater, so we were always kept in food. On my birthday in December, 1971, I sold my camera. The pictures I have are only in my mind now.

We ended up in Bengashi, Libya. There were five of us. Flobird, myself, my sister, my 1 1/2 year old niece, and two male friends. We tried to drive across the Libyan border into Egypt, but they wouldn't let us. So, a few weeks later, us girls got on a boat and went to Egypt, thereby fulfilling Flobird's "go to Egypt by boat" instructions.

Where the money came from was strange. I, as usual, hooked up with one of the men who was taking care of us. He wanted to marry me. In those days (and maybe even now) people in those countries want to marry Americans which gives them a chance to move to other countries. Anyway, this man took me around to his family and friends and told them a story, which to this day I have no clue as to what he said. He would talk to them in Arabic, and they would give me money. I didn't question it, I just accepted my abundance. I believed, and still do today, that God is the Source and people are channels. Eventually there was enough to put Flobird, Marchand, Simone and I on the boat to Egypt.

I say there is a thin line between stupidity and faith, and I've traveled that line. I certainly had faith in Flobird's faith, and she had faith in her "Little Boss". We arrived in Alexandria, Egypt with an American dollar and an Egyptian dollar.

We were in Egypt for three weeks. The adventures we had there could fill many pages. The fellows finally caught up with us. We discovered, after the fact, that we had been sent wires which we never got. Seems the people we were staying with had plans for us that did not include our male friends. By God's grace, the men found us in Cairo and rescued us, though we didn't know we needed rescuing. I've always maintained that if

God could get me out of Egypt, He could get me out of anywhere.

We went back to Germany and caught a military flight back to the States, arriving in California in August of 1972.

I then traveled back and forth across the states on my own going from Hawaii to the East coast and back again several times. Many times Flobird would come to where I was and live with me. When I met my husband, Jim, in April 1977, she came to stay with us in Florida, and together we moved Jim to New Mexico. That was the last time she lived with me or I traveled with her. What follows are actual shared experiences from some of her birds while traveling.

MARCHAND

One night Mom decided to leave Dad, called a taxi, and she, Sis and I went to Sacramento to her mom's. We had a kitty with us which was mine, and we weren't supposed to have it. When the kitty meowed, Mom swore to the cab driver we had no cat. I was scared and giggled because I knew we were doing something against the rules, and I couldn't keep the kitty quiet.

In 1966 when I was 16, I moved to the North Shore of Hawaii where Mom and her husband (at that time) lived. He got drunk, and we had episodes. One time he was chasing her with an ironing board around Combs Court where we lived. I yelled at him. He always looked like a monster to me when he was drinking. I chased him and Mom then got between them, grabbed the ironing board and yanked him down. Shortly afterwards, Mom and I got on a plane and returned to California. We came back to Hawaii two weeks later and moved into a house down the street from him. He sobered up for a few months.

That was Mom's last relationship with a man. She felt he was her soul mate. However, he did not get sober and stay sober while we were there, though he may have in later years.

In 1967 we left Hawaii and moved back to California. I had to finish my junior year. I stayed with Sis for awhile, then with

Mom, but was back with Dad in Riverside, California, before school started. Mom lived in a little apartment above Love's Burgers in Laguna Beach for a couple of months, and then returned to the North Shore on Oahu where she moved into what became known as the God House. She met Tom and Wayne at that time. Tom and his wife Laura (of that time) lived two houses behind. I came back two days after graduation in 1968.

After I returned to Hawaii, we moved to Spencer Park on the Big Island and lived in a van we named Yellow Bird. Doug and David joined us. Doug and I got married in June of 1969. We traveled to Virginia Beach where Doug went into the service (Mom told him that it was God's army and to go be the best soldier he could be), did his basic training in Georgia, and then he and I moved to Oklahoma. Mom went back to Hawaii. (There were so many travels and adventures that it would take an entire book to write about all of them).

I remember being in Israel with Mom and Simone. We lived in a rock structure whose roof was a tarp that was held down by rocks. I was pregnant with Shaylan. Mom and I stayed there while Sis, Doug and David were in town during the week. They'd come out on weekends, and would miss the storms on the Red Sea, and the army guys coming, and making coffee in the wind at 4:30 in the morning. I loved doing that for her. I loved serving her, too. And in my heart, it wasn't a drudgery. It was a joy because I was the only one there. I'd walk, with Simone on my hip, five kilometers to get us water, so she'd have coffee in the morning. We would talk for hours and read and listen. It was quite a growing, mystical time for me.

I remember the first time Doug, David, I and Love, the kitty, traveled across to Virginia Beach and landed with only a dime. We had gone on this toll road (we'd had 35 cents), and we had to put a quarter in this little thing to get through the toll, leaving us with a dime. We pulled in to this parking lot, parked, and went to sleep. The next morning we woke up, and the three of us went out and got a job. That was in August of 1969.

One time we were going across the states, and we ended up in Houston. We looked in phone books for an AA club house. We'd gotten the phone number, and we were out of money, out of gas, and it was 5:00 p.m. We were stopped at this light, and this guy in front of us had a flat tire. David jumped out, helped the guy change his tire, and the guy gave him $2. David asked him in the process of changing the tire where the AA Club was, and he told him how to get there. We walked in, the people there sat us down, and cooked this humongous meal for all of us. We just cried tears of gratitude.

Another time I remember getting on the boat in Libya when Mom, Sis, I, and Simone were going to Egypt, and we were grateful we had one American dollar and 10 Egyptian pesetas. We were smugglers, but we didn't know it. While on the ship, someone came to our cabin and asked Mom if she would take these sweaters and bolt of material to Mohammed in Alexandria, and Mom said, sure. She always accepted her abundance. She kept trying to sell or give away these sweaters. Eventually the person who was to have them, got them. While we were in Alexandria, we were almost sold for white slavery. They loved Simone, because she was blond, and Sis and I because we were American.

A cab driver took us to a person who called himself Jimmie Green. He put us up in this grand hotel that faced the ocean. Each floor was decorated as a different country. We were on the 5th floor which was from England. It was January 2, 1972, and at the end of this hallway, there was a small Christmas tree with the nativity scene. We stood there and cried. The birth of the Christ is not celebrated in Arabic countries.

I never thought about it as following Mom. I didn't feel like I was following her. I felt fortunate that we got to travel together. All I ever wanted to do was travel, go to different places and experience life in different countries. It was like inside myself I'd always wanted to go to Egypt. I'd always wanted to go to all these places since I was a kid. We just got to do it together with her. Most of the time on a wing and a prayer.

Mom was always turning us within to our own hearts. Telling us to listen to OUR hearts. What did our hearts say - not hers. It was April 1972 in Israel. We had discovered that any male child born in Israel would have to return at age 18 to serve in the Israeli army, plus, they were still waiting for the Messiah to come. I was seven months pregnant with Shaylan and knew he was going to be a boy. Sis, Simone and I got on a ship to Greece. Mom, Doug and David would follow as soon as they could.

One month later they found us at a friend's house in Athens, Greece. We had figured I'd have Shaylan on this little wooden bed. The wife was to be the mid-wife. (At eight months pregnant you need to start thinking of these things). Mom, David, and Doug appeared at the door and within a week all of us were on a train back to Kitzigen, Germany.

We had to switch trains in Munich. I recall standing there, all of us reading the signs. We looked like tired street people with all this gear. A train was decided on. Everyone got on the train with all our gear and all of a sudden my heart went nuts. I knew it was the wrong train. I picked up Simone and our gear and got off. Everyone looked at me as if I'd lost my mind. I refused to get on. Mom's heart was very quiet. Full heart, empty think tank. Everyone finally got off the train and no one was real happy with me, until we did find the right train. Mom just smiled.

TOM TOM

I traveled with Flobird but not out of the United States, although I tried. I tried to get to Egypt, and got as far as Rome, Italy. I tried to catch up, but never did.

I traveled from Hawaii to the East Coast and back and forth with her.

Little things stand out, like being away from her when I wasn't living with her, and I'd get these feelings and have to call Flobird. Everyone would kid me about it, but I'd do it and inevitably she'd written in her journal that morning, "Tom Tom is going to call me. It's time to go." And I'd go. See, I knew I was supposed to call her.

One thing I really remember about trusting in God was when Flobird and I left New Mexico in my blue Chevy truck, and we were gone exactly one month. We headed across through Texas to Florida and then ventured up to Virginia Beach. It was a significant time because it was just the two of us. I would pick up work wherever we were, painting, etc. I made about $800 that month which was a lot at that time. I'd drive, and she'd sleep in the back of the truck. I kept her in cigarettes.

One time in Hawaii we were living up on a coffee farm, and Flobird woke up one morning and said, "Well, God said to prepare. I'm leaving today." I remember saying, "Flobird, why? We are just so happy here and so comfortable. This is so neat. Why do we have to leave?" I didn't want to leave. I was comfortable. I figured if we left, we'd end up in a tent or something. All I know is that two to three hours later, we were living in a house on Alii Drive. That is an example of her following that inner feeling. After we walked out the door, and not even knowing where we were going, here I was in what I called the dream house. It was the neatest house I'd ever lived in. Right across the street from the ocean. There were many times Flobird did that. I wouldn't be getting the guidance, so I followed hers.

I did learn how to live without money. Those were the easy days. Now, to have a business and have all this money and play this big monopoly game takes so much energy. I get fearful now, not trusting. So much more so than when I didn't have any money.

KAYE

I traveled with Flobird in the early 1970's in Hawaii. The experience was a lesson in faith. This woman had such a faith in God that everyone who met her was drawn to her. We lived in a park in a milk truck. There were always people there seeking Flobird's counsel. It was wonderful just to listen to her talk about God and love. We had no money but every need was met. When we needed food, it was there. When we needed someone to work on the truck, it was there. I learned to be humble and to receive as well as give.

All her little birds looked after her and gave to her with love, so that her needs were fulfilled while she was doing God's work. Strangers would show up at the right time and place with whatever was needed. The little miracles are too numerous to name. They were a part of daily life.

ANNE

The thing I remember most about Flobird and traveling with her is that she never went anywhere without taking Little Boss with her.

MIKE

I first lived with Flobird at Sunset Beach on the North Shore of Oahu in February, March and April of 1968. We lived on the ocean in a 4 bedroom, 2 bath house. I worked as a teacher in Kaneohe. The Beachcombers Spiritual Progress meeting started there. It was the first AA meeting on the North Shore.

I also lived with Flobird in Kona in 1973 for three months at White Sands Beach Estates. Both were great spiritual experiences for me and highlights of my AA journey. I did visit Flo in Virginia Beach twice in 1975-1976. Short visits of a few days. I never traveled with her, but I visited her in many of the places she traveled.

WAYNE

Traveling with Flobird was always an adventure, and I traveled a lot with her. Around the islands as well as elsewhere. In 1969 Flobird, Marchand, and I took off for Europe. Doug was over there. It's an interesting story, because a couple of things happened. One of them was that my father had died, and I got this small inheritance. Because of my past, I had run up a whole bunch of credit-card bills, taken some money out to get a place for Tom and I, and several other things.

Anyway, this one bill was outstanding. Well, a sum of money came through, and Doug, who was in Germany at that time, was saying he needed help. He was having a hard time with drugs and alcohol. He'd been drafted into the army, and he was married to Marchand. So this money came through, and I felt like, well, Flobird had a prepare to leave this place to go to Germany to help Doug. Marchand was going to go, and I was going to go, but I had this conflict of whether I should pay this outstanding bill or just go to Germany.

There was a lot of validity to do this 12 Step work and make a 12 Step call on Doug at this time, but yet there was this wreckage of my past glaring me in the face about these credit-card bills. If I did pay those credit-card bills off that meant I couldn't go to Germany. It would probably take all the money. Marchand had her way paid because she was married to Doug, and he was in the army, but Flobird and I wouldn't be able to go. So I had a conflict there. It was very easy to rationalize what I wanted to do which was take the money and use it. Your Higher Power wants you to do it this way.

Flobird advised me to follow my heart. Rigorous honesty. She never once thought of herself in a situation like that. So after talking it over with her, I just said, 'Okay, right.' I sat down, and I wrote this letter to this credit-card company, and I said, 'Listen, I owe you guys some money, and I don't know how much it is, but I'd like to pay it off. I'd like to clear my conscious.' It was like an Eigth and Nineth Step. I put the letter in the mail, and gave it up to God and said, 'Okay, whatever. It's not my business. I did the footwork.'

In less than a week I received a letter back, and it said, 'We do not know who you are. We have no record of you. If you have your credit card, give us your number.' Well, I didn't have the credit card. They'd taken it away from me. So that was my answer. They didn't know who I was. I'd made the attempt.

So, consequently, we took the money, and flew from Hawaii to the Mainland. We dinged around, and got a car - one of these Triple A Drive-a-car things. They give you a car to drive, you buy the gas. I wanted to go through South Dakota which turned out to be a big fiasco. We drove across country. We were to take the car was to a place called Luckland, Wisconsin. I'll never forget that place. It was horrible. I stood for eight hours trying to hitch hike on that road. Nobody would pick me up. I had dropped Flobird and Marchand in Minneapolis. They were waiting for me. I waited and waited and waited at the bus depot. I finally got a ride.

When I got to Minneapolis, I was sick. I had taken a shot for small pox, and it had erupted. I'd never in my life had one take, and this one erupted like a balloon. Anyway, we got on this bus, and we got all the way to New York, and got to the airport. There was a military flight leaving, so we grabbed our things, and we barely made this flight. It was incredible.

Flobird ended up with my suitcase, and I ended up with Flobird's suitcase. She and Marchand caught a military flight, and I had to go through this thing called Island Air, and hang out for a day or so to get a cheap flight ($223 to Europe at that time), and it landed in Iceland. You can imagine the humor that went down with me opening my suitcase at Customs.

Anyway, then I had to try to find Flobird and Marchand. We ended up in one of those little countries next to Holland. I had to take a train to Germany, and I knew they were in a place called Kitzigen. It took me a lot of time to find them, but finally I found out where Doug was, and found out where they were staying, and then I found a place to stay. Eventually they came and stayed there too.

Every day I went out looking at houses to rent. Houses were terribly hard to find. We finally found one in Wurzburg which was a 30-40 minute train ride from Kitzigen. I got this house, and Marchand and Flobird settled in. Then I went traveling around Europe, returning every so often to Wurzburg. Cherie came over at one point. I always found it amusing that we all traveled through Spain and down that way, and we were in Cairo, Egypt, at the same exact time, but not together. I always felt that the Higher Power had me there in case I was needed. But everyone seemed to have walked through their own experience without any damage. But when I think back about that time, I always wonder, if something had been happening or started to happen, would we have met on the street? I don't know.

After that, I continued my travels, and so did everyone else. I met Linda in '72, and when we came back from the traveling, Linda met Flobird at Jimmy's house in Los Angeles. After everybody's travels we all moved back to the islands. Linda and I eventually moved down to Naalehu, and life went on.

I always did enjoy my travels with Flobird. There was never any fear. She constantly taught me how to follow my heart. Always. And it's something that I use all the time when working with newcomers. Listen to your heart. Follow your heart. Do what you think is right. It has sustained me all through my travels. Whenever I got down, got depressed, got into a situation that was weird or wonderful, it was always Flobird who was there to help me out. Not in the physical body, but in the spiritual.

7

DYING

So I began my career of following my heart. And everybody would say, "That's impossible, you can't do it." And I'd say, "With God, all things are possible." I found I can keep my head in the clouds, but my feets have to be on the ground.
-- Flobird

CHERIE

I knew Flobird was sick, but I didn't consciously know it was cancer. I always wanted her to go to a doctor, but she had something against doctors and hospitals. I'm sure it was from her past. I knew she was in God's hands. When I found out she was going to die, I felt sad, yet glad. I knew she'd been in pain a long time, and I knew the only way out of it was to leave the body. But I felt scared, too. What would I do without her. She had always been there when I'd had questions about life that no one else seemed to have answers for. However, I think I dealt with her death in April, several months before her death, when she had tried one final time to stop smoking. She put me in charge of her cigarettes, as always, because I was the "strong" one. When I found out she was searching for butts and then smoking them in secret, I cried. I knew then she was going to die. I just didn't know it would be that soon.

Others also knew she was going to die. Many were in tune with her spiritually at the time she was in the hospital. Many learned about her death later.

ELOISE

I always felt she was going to die. When it came, I was numb.

JOY

She was dead when we heard about her illness, and felt the world had lost a special person.

ANNE

From 1976 to 1978, I spent a lot of time at Estero Beach. We have a lot of Sea Gulls here, and it could have been July 16, 1978 when about 15 or more sea gulls were flying all around in front of my motel home. They seemed very happy and free. I remember thinking about Flobird.

KAYE

When I heard of Flobird's death, it was hard to believe because she had accepted life so many times when others would have given in to death. She had no fear of death. I knew she was at last free of her weak and painful body. But it was very hard for me to let go. When Marchand told me the details of her death, I just had tears of joy and faith and amazement at this woman's life of love. I see her flying free like all the birds she loved so much all her life. I see her smiling bigger than ever and those brown eyes shining so brightly.

HAROLD

I learned about her death after the fact and felt a loss, and a great sadness. I know she still lives.

GOLDENEAGLE

I learned that Flobird was going to die just about exactly one year before she did. I had traveled to the Land in New Mexico via LA/Phoenix and arrived sometime in late June. I remember going in to see her after we arrived. She was laying on a big bed and smoking. She remarked that she'd be gone (dead) in about a year. I don't remember exactly how she said it. But the message was clear to me. That was the last time I saw her.

MIKE

I was living in Los Angeles, California. I knew she was sick from the frequent coughing on her letter tapes to me. It seemed like a time of isolation for Flo. I knew she would not go to a doctor unless forced. Shortly afterwards, I had a phone call from Doug that she was in Texas and had only a short time to live because of advanced lung cancer. Doug invited me to stay with his parents, so I flew to Texas to see Flo. I knew her feelings on death and dying and was in full accord with her beliefs. I cried, and I was in a low emotional place at that time. I did not feel deep grief, but I felt an understanding of her own words to me about death.

WAYNE

When I learned she was going to die, there was sadness, but not a sadness for me because I knew she was always there if I needed her. I could always contact Flobird. I always knew Flobird was around, and I could always find her no matter what was coming down.

I was in the hospital at this time under a tremendous amount of pain after surgery, and I knew they were going to need to administer pain killers. I used to talk to Flobird. I felt her there when I needed it. They had given me all these Percadans to take, and when I came home, I took one, but I hated the whole feeling, so I got up out of my bed and flushed them down the toilet. It was totally ludicrous. I learned to live with the pain. To transmute it. It's been that way ever since.

There was not a sadness when I learned she was dying. I knew she was ready. It just felt right. I knew she had come to earth for a reason. The Higher Power had used her to plant the seeds of love and service to those people around her. It's been proven out today because the people with whom she was directly involved, every one of us, is still involved in and working the Program to one extent or another. So I wasn't that crushed when I heard she was going to die.

I would have liked to have been there to talk to her in person, but I was there in spirit. She was there. She came to me when I was in the hospital. I felt her presence.

It seemed like Flobird hung onto life that last year waiting for both Marchand and I to be married and settled. On the other hand, other's couldn't meet anyone until Flobird left.

TOM TOM

I thought I was supposed to be with Flobird, and would not allow myself to get involved in anything else. My feeling when she died was relief. I was free to go out and be me. I was cut loose. She didn't do that to me. I did that. I tied myself to her.

Since her death, my whole life has been based on what I learned from her. I have to practice meditation. My spiritual belief I learned from her, watching her live. I'll never forget her. I never stop talking about her. Yet I'm free, doing things I probably would have felt guilty about doing when she was alive. Like having a business, having a nice home, being married. Not walking around in a loin cloth. I thought I had to walk around in a loin cloth. That was MY interpretation of it. So, basically, the whole concept of putting God first, and inviting others into my life, having my house open to others, all that stuff is totally from Flobird.

CHERIE

My sister and I and our families were living in Grants, New Mexico when Flobird entered the hospital in Cleburne, Texas. We got a phone call from Tom to let us know of a pending operation she was to have. I had just begun a job as a waitress on the graveyard shift, and I quit because I had no idea how long we would be gone. Marchand and I left as soon as we could after the phone call, drove 12 hours straight to arrive in Cleburne the day before she was to have the operation. They were going to remove a lung that was full of cancer.

MARCHAND

The day before she had her operation, before Sis and I came to the hospital, Tom called, and said, "Marchand, your mother is going to have an operation tomorrow to remove her lung." Then he put her on the phone. I remember talking to her, and all I wanted her to tell me was that she needed me. She finally told me, but it was in this all inclusive esoteric thing that was always there. All I wanted to do was be her daughter for a minute, and have her tell me that she needed me to be there. And that was always an issue with us because it was real important to me.

I asked her if she needed me, and she said, "Of course I need you. I need everybody." She named everybody off. I said, "Wait a minute. Mom, this is your daughter. This is Marchand, and I realize that I'm just an extension and a part of you, and I belong to life, but do you need ME to be there?" She finally said yes.

We drove 12 hours straight, and I remember walking in to her room after we arrived and trying real hard not to cry. I didn't let go. I didn't cry. I stopped any feeling that was there. She hugged me and held my hand and introduced me to her nurse.

I stayed at the hospital. There had been another lady there, and she went for an operation, but she didn't come back. Mom said she thought something must have happened to the lady. I ended up sleeping in that bed. The hospital let me have that bed for the two weeks we were there. Mom and I talked and listened and were just together in those two weeks.

Mom would give me her food and tell me I'd have to eat, and I'd say, "Mom, YOU have to eat," and I would feed her. She'd hand me the menu and ask me to pick out the food because she wasn't planning on eating it.

I went back to New Mexico before Sis did. I drove her truck, and she came back with Doug's brother, David.

CHERIE

Marchand spent most of the time at the hospital for those two weeks, but I did stay now and then. The one thing that stands out in my mind was Flobird getting up in the middle of the night this one night, trying to go to the bathroom without asking for help. She was very stubborn that way sometimes. She tried to walk to the bathroom by hanging onto the side of her bed, but when she reached the end of her bed, she fell down. She was bound and determined to do it herself. I was asleep but woke up at the sound of the crash. I sat up and saw her lying on the floor. Getting her up and into the bathroom was a challenge because she fought me all the way. I begged her to please not try to do that by herself again. She really didn't want to have to depend on anyone. She wanted to be able to take care of herself, but she couldn't, and she felt powerless. She didn't like that at all.

I remember being disgusted with those that came in to see her. They wanted her to listen to them while they shared their problems. I wanted to say, "Why can't you guys give instead of get?!" But I know that WAS giving to her. That's what kept her alive.

TOM TOM

I came to Texas twice when she was dying. The first time, I walked into the hospital room, saw her, and I broke down crying. I hadn't seen her in a few months. I had to go outside. The reality hit me. I felt so bad because I had some of my own petty little problems going on at that time, and had to take her time and talk to her about it.

Larry and I took turns taking care of her at night at the hospital. After I returned to New Mexico, Flobird was released from the hospital and went to stay at Doug's parents.

Right before Flobird went to Cleburne, she had gone from Oahu to the Big Island. She was always coughing, and we knew she was sick, but we didn't know it was that bad. I had a job going and had some money. Flobird called and wanted to go to Texas, and for the first time ever, I didn't want to send all my money. You see, usually when it came to our group, I always gave all my money away. I just didn't care. So this is where the guilt came, 'cause it was the first time I ever felt rebellious about it. Anyway, Tom and I both took on the burden, and we split the ticket for her. After I found out she went to Texas and was dying, and it was the last time she'd asked for money, I went through this rebellious thing. So I really had a lot of guilt feelings behind that. It was the one and only time I wanted to refuse her.

I returned to New Mexico, picked up my kids, then hitchhiked back to Texas. I was there with her right up to when we took her back to New Mexico. Larry and I left first to help work on the house and get the extra room ready before she arrived.

TOM

Of course all through the years that I knew her, she was in so much pain physically, and there was nothing we could do. When someone would come around and ask for help, we'd watch her come out and help. She could be on the ground sobbing in just so much pain, and yet a person would come to see her, and they would never know how much pain she was in. She was unbelievable in that way. Something we'd see over and over again in her.

I think we all had respect for her. We'd take care of her, take her coffee, and people on the outside would see it as powerful mind control stuff - influencing these lost little souls. What they didn't know was the tremendous respect we had for Flobird and the admiration we had for her as a human being. She had love and compassion for people. It was a privilege to serve her, take care of her, watch over her.

Of course, another phenomenal thing about her was that she never expected it. She never asked for much of anything. I'm so amazed still. I'm not that present for people. There are still people that come into my life, and I go, 'Come on God, please. Not this one.' I know Flobird used to say that too. But when they would walk into the door, she'd be totally there for them. I guess that's the way I am with people, too. I don't reject people. I don't scare anybody away or tell them I don't have the time. I do show up. But not at the level she did.

All of us really became more independent then. It was a shift in the group, in all of us. It was a good shift. It was preparing us for her leaving.

I think for as long as I knew Flobird, she was not in good shape physically. It wouldn't have surprised me to walk into her room or tent to find she had passed on. She virtually lived on toast, baked beans, mayonnaise and cigs. I think all of us were prepared for her dying. We just didn't know when.

So when we finally got word that she was in Texas and in the hospital, and they had opened her up and discovered she had cancer all over her body, I think we were prepared for that. We were more prepared than she was. She had this tremendous faith in the here and now that she didn't project about stuff like that.

We went to Texas to see her. Got to the hospital, walked in the room, and seeing her laying there in a comatose state, I know that Tom Tom started crying. I don't think I really cried about Flobird. I wanted to help her in any way I could to make the transition.

I was sitting there next to her holding her hand, and it was very quiet in the room, and she was kinda comatose, making sounds, and noises, and suddenly she began touching my hand with her hand, squeezing it, and she says, "Who is this?" I said, "Flobird, it's me, Tommy McCall." And she goes, "Tommy, Tommy, for god's sake when are you going to get honest with yourself!" I just about shit. It was classic Flobird. She would come out of nowhere and hit you right between the eyes. I said, "Flobird, I've come a long ways." And she said, "You sure have, baby. You've come a long, long ways."

Then I remember Doug coming to the other side of her holding her hand. She squeezed his hand and said, "Who's this?" He said, "It's me; it's Doug." Doug started sobbing and crying. He had his head on her stomach, and she says, "Baby, it's okay, Baby, it's okay. You made it just under the wire."

She laid there for another day or so, in that half in and half out of the comatose state, and I remember her moaning and making sounds, and the phone would ring, and it was Tony from Virginia, and he'd say, "How is she?" And I'd say, "She's just layin' here. She's quiet. But we'll put the phone up to her ear, and you can say something to her, Tony."

It was just amazing. We put the phone to her ear, and Tony would say something to her, and she would start talking - coherently talking. "Hi, Baby. How ya doin', Sweetheart? Yeah, I love you, too, Sweetheart. How ya doin'? How's your lust? Give it up to God, Baby. Yeah, that's right. I've been through worse than this. Don't worry about me. I'm doin' fine.

I love you Sweetheart. Bye, bye."

I can remember several phone calls coming in from around the country, and she would be out of body, and the minute the phone was at her ear, there she would be. Classical Flobird. She would be present. There was a spirit inside that woman that was beyond the flesh. At that time it was so clear who was running that woman. It wasn't this person we saw and touched and looked at. There was something much more powerful there.

There were days when she was sitting up, and we'd come walking into the room. I'll never forget this. She was sitting there with a cigarette in her hand, and she said, "Look it Tommy, I finally stopped smoking. I CAN'T smoke. Look it what happens." And she would suck on the cigarette and blow it right out of her mouth. She couldn't suck it into her throat. She couldn't inhale it. And she was so happy about the fact that she couldn't inhale anymore, and then she'd keep smoking. It was unbelievable. A rebel.

CHERIE

The doctor performed the operation, however, he did not remove the lung because he discovered her entire body was riddled with cancer. He just closed her back up, and told us she had about a month to live. This one particular night there were about 15 of us at the hospital. It was about 1:30 a.m. Against all hospital rules the night nurse let us remain. She felt she owed it to Flobird because thanks to Flobird's gentle, loving way, she was finally able to forgive and release her own mother who had died recently of cancer.

Both Marchand and I felt Flobird was going to die this particular evening. I went out to the waiting room and told everyone, and so one by one we came in, stood by her bedside, and said our good-byes.

MARCHAND

I stood in the room behind the bed with my fingers rubbing her temples over her head at the point in time when everyone was filtering in. I was telling her to follow the Christ pure light, and she kept saying, "It's so beautiful here. It is so beautiful. And look! They're calling me. They're calling me. I'm going. Okay, I'm going." I felt as if we'd done this before. Like I had guided her through this transition many, many years ago.

It was as if I walked down this pathway with her to where all these people were calling her, and all of a sudden she said, "They're healing me. They're healing me." And this feeling of hope went through me as if, God, we're going to have a miracle healing. Her body is going to be healed. I knew it inside. And then, I knew that wasn't true, that she wasn't going to be physically healed. They were preparing the silver cord to make the transition to the other side smooth. She kept saying, "It's so beautiful, and they're calling me to come." At this time the room was filled with a glowing peace. Then all of a sudden I felt her snap right back into her body. She exclaimed, "I'm not ready yet. I'm not going yet. No matter what. It's not time!" Everyone had gone.

The doctors came in the next morning and said we'd given her something.

TOM

She got really, really bad again. Cherie and Marchand called us up late at night and said, "If you want to say your good-byes, then this is the time to do it 'cause we don't expect her to live through the night."

So we all went down to the hospital somewhere around 11:00 PM. There were quite a few of us. Don't remember how many. We were all in the hospital room. It was so quiet in the room. You could hear her breathing. Just barely breathing. You could just sense the life force leaving her. Each one of us went up to her to say our good-byes, and we each gave her a kiss. She was out of it, but she was coherent in the sense that she would say good-bye back, or just squeeze our hand, or say, "I love you, Sweetheart. Bye, bye, I love you." It was so sweet.

We all left and came back in the morning to the hospital.

There she was - sitting up in bed talking to two nurses about writing out their Fourth Steps and she'd take the Fifth Step with them. You could see the light in the eyes of the nurses. There she was again. Classical Flobird.

8

RETURN TO THE ENCHANTED FOREST

AA is a lot like golf. You have to hit your own ball. You have to improve your own game. Nobody can do it for you.
-- Flobird

CHERIE

I never felt that need to take care of her. I followed her. I wanted what she had, and I figured she had the faith in God, and if I hung out close enough to her, I'd get it some where along the line. Seeing her in this state was very hard. Shortly after she came out of the hospital, she decided she wanted to die in New Mexico on the land in the Enchanted Forest as she called it.

Tom called on Thursday, July 13th to say she had asked for a minister and that she wanted to return to New Mexico. Marchand and I left around 3:00 PM for Cleburne and arrived in Texas at 7:00 AM on Friday the 14th.

We brought her back to New Mexico on Saturday, July 15th. Driving from Texas to New Mexico was quite an experience. Before we left Texas, Flobird said she wanted to die clean and sober. She said, "I will only take what pills were prescribed." That is all she wanted. "I don't care what I say to you, don't give me any more!"
As always, she put me in charge.

It took us 12 hours to drive from New Mexico to Texas, 19 hours to return. We stopped what felt like 100 times so she could pee, and the pain she felt as she tried to get in and out of the International showed on every character wrinkle on her face. But when she'd ask for a pain pill, I'd tell her no if it wasn't time for one, just like she told me to. She got so angry with me, she quit talking to me.

We stopped in Amarillo, Texas, to eat. I asked her if she wanted anything. She said, "No, I'm not hungry." We went in, ate, came back out, and Flobird ranted and raved at us for not loving her. We didn't care about her because we wouldn't bring her any food.

When we were within a few miles of the land, she began telling us we didn't love her because we wouldn't give her any pills, but Larry loved her and he would take care of her. I didn't take anything she said to heart. I knew it was because of the pain, and the situation.

On the final mile, while driving up the bumpy hill to the land, she kept yelling at me, "You're trying to kill me!" I remember yelling back, "Mother, I'm not trying to kill you. You're dying." She absolutely refused to talk to me. She only wanted Larry because Larry loved her and cared how she felt. So, when we arrived, I turned her over to Larry. Later on, when she was in the rented hospital bed in the newly finished room in Tom's house that was built especially for her, she apologized for what she said.

MARCHAND

The doctors said she would never make the trip. They released her and figured she would die before she ever reached New Mexico.

TOM

We all went back to New Mexico, and Flobird went to Cleburne. And she was on the heavy narcotics but didn't want to be. She cut them out, and then got up one night to go to the bathroom and fell and broke her ribs and was in tremendous pain again, and from then on she just got worse. Then we had the word from her. She said, "I'm not supposed to die here in Texas. I'm supposed to die in New Mexico. Come and get me."

Cherie and Marchand took off for Texas to pick her up. Meanwhile, we needed a place for her. I was originally planning on building an addition to our house. I had the foundation laid out already. When they left to pick Flobird up, we started building. It took us 2 1/2 days to build this room. Morning, noon, and night. But as Marchand and Cherie pulled up with Flobird, the room was completed. We had already rented a hospital bed from the hospital. We had the entire room built, roofed, carpeted, pictures on the walls, flowers. We had left the one side of the wall opened without any studs, put the hospital bed in the room, picked up Flobird and moved her into the bed. Then we closed the wall up.

She was such a little child in some ways. She was saying, "Amazing. Look at this. Amazing. You're a trip, God." It was like an instant room for Flobird. Got her all settled in and then made some plans about how we were going to keep a vigil watch on her. She went through the night, and the next day, but in the afternoon, I went upstairs to lay down for a little bit and fell asleep.

TOM TOM

Flobird arrived back at the land at noon on Saturday, and we put her in the house by 3:00 P.M. I woke up the next morning, and I knew in my gut that I had to leave New Mexico. I talked to Larry about it. I didn't know what to do. I felt like I had to leave, but I was with Larry who was driving. He was okay if we stayed or left. We didn't know if Flobird was going to live another month, another 6 months, another day. We had no idea. All I knew was that I knew I had to go that day. And I felt this feeling that if I left before Flobird died, I would never forgive myself. But I was so torn because my gut said I had to leave, so I didn't know what to do.

MARCHAND

When she was settled into the room, I went in to see her. She took my hand and said, "It's right. God said it was right." She was very calm and at peace. It was time for her to go. She was telling us that love is the answer and the way to go. That it was right, that God meant for two people to be together, and that marriage was good in His love. She thanked Don and she thanked Jim. She told us that it was okay, and not to forget about the rainbow. She said, "Remember the rainbow and watch for the rainbow." And that was real significant later.

TOM TOM

So, this is what actually happened. We were all in her room, and she was breathing very heavy. She kinda fell asleep with all of us in there. So we all left the room. I went and sat in a chair in the room next door. There was a window looking into her room. I remember sitting there with my eyes closed. I began meditating and pictured her lying there surrounded by light. All of sudden the light surrounded her body, and there was a channel; it wasn't closed at the head. As I sat there, I saw her astral body take off. I saw her float right up and out of her body. She was dressed in white with her Love That Red lipstick on and she looked real pretty. As that happened, every hair on my body stood on end. I went numb. When I got up and looked in the window, there was a mist in there. I didn't know what was going on. Unbelievable. I was just numb. I got right up and walked in her room and she was gone. She had died.

I ran out yelling, "Flobird's gone."

The funny part is that I WAS supposed to leave that day. Larry and I just picked up and left, but as we left we looked back and saw this rainbow surrounding the entire 30 acres of land.

MARCHAND

I knew she was going to leave that day. I knew when she held my hand and looked in my eyes with love and gratitude that she would leave the body that day. I said leave the body because I couldn't say die. I said for a long time, she left her body. I couldn't accept that she died. That was too final.

She let me know that she was proud of us, her children and birds and felt safe for us to stay here. That her journey on earth was finished; that we must travel our own pathways. "Think of me and I will be there," she said. "Watch for the rainbow."

Mom departed about 4:00 PM on Sunday, July 16. I remember Tom yelling my name out, and then I came running down the hill, and threw myself over her and kissed her and crying, said, "You're free, you're free, and you don't have to hurt anymore."

Tom and Larry left immediately after she died as we had no phone to call the coroner. They went to Ice Caves to call. It took about an hour before the Coroner came to pronounce her dead of natural causes.

I remember feeling that I didn't want them to take her away.

When they did, we stood around wondering, now what do we do. It was life as usual. Clean the new room, cook dinner.

TOM

It was Tom Tom's watch. He was downstairs. He had that experience of seeing her walking past him in the white gown with the silver cord from her head, and he ran in and she was gone. She had left the body.

I remember all of us coming in to the room. Cherie and Marchand went in and fixed her up. Put her Love That Red lipstick on. Combed her hair. So sweet, so loving.

I realized one of the most important people in my life had just gone on. I was happy for her. I hadn't even dealt with the sense of my own loss that she was gone. I just remember thinking that this was Cherie and Marchand's mom, and they were taking care of her, saying good bye to her. It was a very tender moment.

We got the Coroner to come up and get the body. I remember the Coroner came, and they didn't know what to think about us. They didn't know how long the body had been there.

MARCHAND

At about 6:30 PM a young man came walking toward us. He was seeking the Beachcombers Spiritual Progress Group. He had read about us in the Grapevine and was hoping he'd found a meeting. We all looked at each other, explained why we weren't having one, then decided that it was the best reason to have one.

As the saying goes, "When anyone anywhere reaches out their hand for help, I want the hand of AA always to be there, and for that, I am responsible."

We held the meeting in the new room. We sat in a circle around the room. I sat at the foot of the bed facing this huge picture window from which we could see the land. We started out reading all the normal stuff. I got to read How It Works and in the middle of it I looked up. In the window was this most brilliant rainbow I ever remember seeing. It seemed to be pulsating with life, with love, reaching out to us. I stopped reading and pointed to the rainbow.

My heart was sad and joyous at the same time. Goodbye Mom. You said for us to watch.

Tom called from California the next day. They had been driving at least three hours when we saw the rainbow, and out of his mouth came, "Did you see the rainbow?"

TOM

We stood around in the court yard, and we heard this voice say, "Hey, hi!" There's this guy with a pack on his back, walking up on this little hill behind Marchand and Don's house saying, "Hi, my name is Jerry. I read an article in the AA Grapevine about this group. This Beachcombers Spiritual Progress Traveling group that meets up here on Sunday afternoons, and was wondering if you guys were still having a meeting up here."

He was traveling across country and made a note that he wanted to attend this meeting, and it just so happened he was there that Sunday afternoon. Sunday afternoon was traditionally the time we always had the meeting. And we looked at the guy, and we looked at each other and said, "Yea, sure. We sure are. Why not."

It was kind of a tribute to Flobird. I don't think we would have had the meeting had this guy not walked up. It was an incredible tribute to Flobird. What her life was all about. Birds walking out of the bushes. And she'd be there for them. They'd find her somehow. The meeting was a calm meeting. We all shared some of our feelings about Flobird. I don't think it had really sunk in for us yet. We were all still very peaceful.

Jerry left. A month or so later we got a letter from him and he said, "I don't know who this woman was, this Flobird who died, but something happened to me at that meeting, that afternoon, and I haven't been the same since."

That was what she was about. She changed people's lives. You just came into her presence, and your life was changed. She didn't have to do a whole lot or say a whole lot.

She just kinda had that Cinderella dust that she'd sprinkle wherever she went. People would wake up. She gave us good disciplines. Particularly about her dying. She said, "Just let me go. Please, just let me go. Don't have seances, don't do this, don't do that. Don't entrap my spirit. Let me go."

MARCHAND

It was selfish of me to feel any kind of remorse about her going. That was my whole deal in life, not to be selfish. Mom played a very significant part in my life to show me where if I was selfish, God wouldn't love me. She didn't give me that, but that's what I had throughout my life. I wanted to be perfect - not be selfish, think of others, always put others first. You go ten paces if you're only asked to go two. No matter what it is. And that's how I've lived my life.

I was just grateful that she didn't have to hurt anymore. I don't think I cried again until three days later.

CHERIE

Marchand and I stood in the room after she died and asked her spirit what she wanted to wear. We both got white and picked a white Muu Muu from Hawaii. We combed her hair, and tried to put her Love That Red lipstick on her. I say tried because putting lipstick on a lip that has no resistance makes for quite an adventure. I had to wipe her face because I'd smeared the lipstick more than once. By the time the mortuary came to pick her up, she was dressed as Marchand and I had sensed she wanted.

We visited her at the Mortuary before they took her to Albuquerque to be cremated. The mortuary did not expect all of us to appear. They dressed her for us, totally against mortuary rules, then allowed us to go in and say goodbye. Simone laid a white rose in her hands.

9

THE FUNERAL

We have to either sober up, flip our lids permanently, or go to the next plane of existence.

-- Flobird

On July 16, 1978, at 4:00 p.m. Flobird left this plane of existence. She was surrounded by her two daughters, her grandchildren, and many of her birds. Her body was cremated, and her ashes were spread in the mystical enchanted forest of her beloved land at Hidden Valley Spiritual Community, Ice Caves, New Mexico. A funeral was held under the Ponderosa pines in a pavilion-like structure that was built for her. Those who couldn't be there in the physical sent letters and supported the passing in spirit.

TONY

My heart weeps today because I must accept that I will never see that smiling face again. Yet at the same time I rejoice in knowing she no longer suffers, and she is free at last. This morning in mediation my heart was heavy, and I was thinking about all of you. The tears flowed, and I know that at last the finale has come. Yet the real end is a new beginning towards a greater expression of that love without a price tag. She was sent here to earth to do a job, and she, as a channel, did it in a beautiful way. I know that without that channel, I would not be where I am today.

When this all started, I really wanted to be there, but Flobird's words kept coming to me. "Look forward to those things which are ahead, and let go of those things which are behind.

The ultimate has occurred, and for this minute I feel so alone. Not as alone as I would have felt if Flobird hadn't told me to find my God within. She was so unselfish, yet so human. I don't know why I am writing this, but obviously I need to. She taught me that laughter was a great healer, and it would at times be the only saving grace. I'm going to miss the old body and raised eyebrows, but I shall never forget the memories and the beautiful feelings that I shall carry with me lifetime after lifetime.

My parents and I send our love to all of you and thank you for your lives and the life of Flobird Johnson.

CHERIE

July 23, 1978   4:00 p.m.

We sat around in a circle on the plywood floor of the partially built pavilion with the Ponderosa Pines surrounding us. The sky was filled with clouds as if it, too, were mourning the passing of a dear friend. Everyone joined hands, bowed their heads in silence, then joined together in prayer.

"God, grant me the Serenity to Accept the things I cannot change, the Courage to change the things I can, and the Wisdom to know the difference."

The service was opened in the following manner:

We are gathered here today to pay tribute to Flobird. She was a woman, a mother, a friend. She was a sponsor, a spiritual advisor, an able example to all of us of what love without a price tag is all about. The following statement in its simplicity brings it into focus for all of us and anyone who knew her.

Before I met you I was me without you, and now that we have met, I am me with you added to me, and I have grown. Thank you.

I'd like to read her favorite passage in the Bible. She lived by these words and showed us all that we, too, could put it into living practice.

Matthew 6: 25-34 -

25: "I tell you therefore, do not worry about your living, what you are to eat or drink, or about your body, what you are to wear. Is not the life more important than its nourishment and the body than its clothing?

26: "Look at the birds of the air, how they neither sow nor reap nor gather into barns, but your heavenly Father feeds them. Are not you more valuable than they?

27: "Furthermore, who of you is able through worrying to add one moment to his life's course.

28: "And why worry about clothes? Observe carefully how the field lilies grow. They neither toil nor spin,

29: "but I tell you that even Solomon in all his splendor was never dressed like one of these.

30: "But if God so clothes the grass of the field that exists today and is thrown into the furnace tomorrow, will He not more surely clothe you of little faith?

31: "Do not, then, be anxious, saying, 'What shall we eat?' or 'What shall we drink?' or 'What are we to wear?'

32: "For on all these things pagans center their interest while your heavenly Father knows that you need them all.

33: "But you, seek first His kingdom and His righteousness and all these things will be added to you.

34: "Do not worry therefore, in view of tomorrow, for tomorrow will have its own anxieties. Each day's peculiar troubles are sufficient for it."

A few of us have written briefly what she meant to us, shared with us, gave to us. We'll go around and each one read his own.

(I'm sorry to say the only copy I kept was what I, myself, wrote and read that day.)

To Mom   July 19, 1978
The day did come for you to leave this earthly life behind.
All tasks fulfilled, amends were made,
there's nothing left to bind.
And so you went back to your "home" to see what there is to see.
You may return, or you may not. You'll know what is to be.
There are no words that can express
all that you brought my way.
Without your loving, guiding hand, in darkness I would stay.
You walked beside me in my hate and helped me to let go.
You showed me how to use my wings, and let my insides flow.
You went before to show me how the road of life could be.
If I would give, and love, and share,
I, too, could then be free.
I thank you, Mom, for all that you

have shared with me this life.
For walking with me in my love and being there in strife.
I love you, Mom. I love you much.
I'm glad I came through you.
I hope someday we meet again to share a life brand new.
Although you are not here in form, your spirit lingers on.
You'll always be my guiding light from darkness into dawn.

Another passage from the Bible I'd like to read is Corinthians 13: 1-13

1: "Even though I speak in human and angelic language and have not love, I am as noisy brass or a clashing cymbal.

2: "And although I have the prophetic gift and see through every secret and through all that may be known, and have sufficient faith for the removal of mountains, but I have no love, I am nothing.

3: "And though I give all my belongings to feed the hungry and surrender my body to be burned, but I have no love, I am not in the least benefited.

4: "Love endures long and is kind: love is not jealous: love is not out for display:

5: "It is not conceited or unmannerly; it is neither self-seeking nor irritable, nor does it take account of a wrong that is suffered.

6: "It takes no pleasure in injustice but sides happily with truth.

7: "It bears everything in silence, has unquenchable faith, hopes under all circumstances, endures without limit.

8: "Love never fails. As for prophesying, they will pass away; as for tongues, they will cease; as for knowledge, it will lose its meaning.

9: "For our knowledge is fragmentary and so is our prophesying.

10: "But when the perfect is come then the fragmentary will come to an end.

11: "When I was a child I talked like a child. I thought like a child. I reasoned like a child, but on becoming a man I was through with childish ways.

12: "For now we see indistinctly in a mirror, but then face to face. Now we know partly, but then we shall understand as completely as we are understood.

13: "There remain then, faith, hope, love, these three; but the greatest of these is love."

For the past 18 years, Flobird was an alcoholic before she was anything else. She never forgot where she came from, or where she was going. She helped many of us here and so many more all over the world wake up to life. I think it's only fitting that to bring this to a close, we should read one of her favorite paragraphs from the Big Book of Alcoholics Anonymous found on page 164 in the chapter, A Vision For You:

"Our book is meant to be suggestive only. We realize we know only a little. God will constantly reveal more to you and to us. Ask Him in your morning meditation what you can do each day for the man who is still sick. The answers will come if your own house is in order. But obviously you cannot transmit something you haven't got. See to it that your relationship with Him is right, and great events will come to pass for you and countless others. This is the Great Fact for us.

"Abandon yourself to God as you understand God. Admit your faults to Him and to your fellows. Clear away the wreckage of your past. Give freely of what you find and join us. We shall be with you in the Fellowship of the Spirit, and you will surely meet some of us as you trudge the Road of Happy Destiny.

"May God bless you and keep you--until then."

As tears were shed unashamedly by everyone, Marchand and I opened the can that held her ashes. We were both surprised to see that there were bits and pieces of bones among the ashes. As we walked around the outside of the pavilion, we shook the ashes out of the can. When the can was empty, we joined hands with everyone else.

Let's take a moment for silence, and then pray the Lord's

Prayer:

"Our Father, Who art in Heaven, hollowed be Thy name. Thy kingdom come, Thy will be done, on earth as it is in Heaven. Give us this day our daily bread. Forgive us our trespasses as we forgive those who trespass against us. Leave us not in temptation, but deliver us from evil. For Thine is the Kingdom, and the Power and the Glory, forever. Amen."

10

THE HERE AND NOW

It takes guts to stay sober. Anybody can pick up a drink.
-- Flobird

CHERIE

Even though Flobird died in 1978, she is very much a part of my life today. Probably because she was my mom, and because I believe in many of the things she read and taught. Some of her spiritual teachers like Joel S. Goldsmith are MY spiritual teachers. I find myself reading many of the books she read. Every day I understand more of what she taught while she was alive.

For 14 years after her death I continued to keep the Beachcombers Spiritual Progress meeting going. Wherever I lived, I started it up. I somehow felt obligated to do that. It was like a tradition of the family. But I finally passed it on to someone else, and to my knowledge, it still happens on Sunday afternoons somewhere in the world. At this present writing there is a meeting online called the Beachcombers Spiritual Progress Cyber Group. Many of the beginning members and those who joined later are once again connected to each other.

Many of the things I share with others are things she shared with me. What I am today is primarily because of what she was. She was a great influence on my life, and by writing this, I see how much of me is her, and how much she continues to influence every aspect of my life.

I'm not the only one who continues to be affected by her lasting presence. Many people have communicated with her through their dreams and automatic writing. Even today she is still helping her birds with broken wings fly once more.

ELOISE

She remains a touchstone for love without a price tag.

ANNE

Flobird has deeply affected my life since 1965, and she will continue to until I leave my physical body. Flobird taught me to live, love, laugh and be happy. To share my good fortune with those less fortunate. Accept God's love and abundance.

Flobird: A Bird's Eye View

When I'm unhappy, it's because I'm trying to get instead of give. There is no happiness in getting or having anything. Only in giving. We never die. We live, and live, and live; reincarnation and soul growth; to grow spiritually and walk in the footsteps of Jesus. What would "Little Boss" do? I still try to live my life the way Flobird taught me. Tain't easy, but I keep on keeping on.

KAYE

The seed that Flobird planted in me 32 years ago continues to grow today. It has enabled me to find my own path. The power within that she revealed to me has gotten me through some seemingly impossible times in my life.

Because of her I realize that things happen for a reason, to help me grow and become more enlightened. Without her loving guidance, I might have become bitter and weak. I think of Flobird all the time and know that her spirit is still flying around happy and free. Loving every person including me. I can think of her if I'm afraid and know what she would say to me. In this way I can communicate with her whenever I want to. She continues to be an instrument of God as she was here on earth.

HAROLD

The experiences and things I learned with Flobird will continue to be part of my life for eternity.

GOLDENEAGLE

Often I feel her faith; her demonstrations of that faith; her willingness to love and serve; her trust in God and willingness to do His will. Practicing the Eleventh and Twelfth Steps. She helped me to set a spiritual foundation that to this day supports me when all else seems to fail. Recalling her life and my short time with her and with others since, has often only increased the faith, strength, and direction I feel I often need to take. They were given so long ago and yet work to this day.

She has continued to inspire me and others, as I recall some of the stories I heard and knew of then, and the life I actually experienced with her and the group at that time.

MIKE

Every day her thoughts are with me. The spiritual teachings, the love, understanding, gratitude, and acceptance kept me sober and alive. I loved her as a friend, and as a teacher. We were close to the same age, and I remember her telling me at Sunset Beach that we were sisters in a past life and very, very close.

TOM

Flobird gave me tremendous courage in my own life to share myself. It's automatic to share anything, no matter where I am. She was an example, she showed me how important it was to stay real.

CHERIE

On November 30, 1978, shortly after Flobird died, my sister's house, which was located on the Land at Ice Caves Road in New Mexico, burnt down. Marchand had kept the majority of Flobird's tapes, books, journals, memorabilia. Several of us had planned to build a structure to house these items, so others could come and listen, read, and experience Flobird via these items. While I was driving to Grants, the town located 30 miles away, I was reflecting on how everything that was in the house had burnt within 30 minutes including all of the special bits and pieces of Flobird we were saving. While I was driving, I felt her in the car sitting next to me, and she said, "That's all right. I didn't want a shrine built for me anyway." Granted, I WAS alone, but I would swear she was sitting in the car with me. I heard her speak very clearly.

Flobird always said, "I am only a thought away." And when I need direction, I've often asked myself, "What would Flobird do in this situation?" Sometimes I wish she were here in body, so I could have a one on one conversation with her.

She was always able to tune into whatever problem I had or straighten out my crazy thinking. I think I've missed her most when I'm feeling alone in my spiritual quest. Often it seems there is no one around with similar experiences that I can share. So I keep reading and studying my spiritual teachers in book form. They know and understand, because they have been there.

When I see her handwriting on something, I get all warm and fuzzy inside. Flobird used to say, "If you want to speak to someone who is dead, just pick up your spiritual phone. When you talk to me on the physical phone, you can't see my body. Well, talking to someone who has died is no different. You can't see their body either, but you CAN hear them."

ANNE

Flobird has communicated with me many times through automatic writing for the past 10 years. I can hear from Flobird with my pencil. The words come very fast. I feel that this is truly from the spirit world. I just close my eyes and think of Flobird or anyone else who is in the spirit world and let the pencil go.

(Message sent with the letter)
"Hi Annie Oakley. I love you. You are beautiful. I am your eternal sponsor. I am so happy for Cherie, my fantastic daughter, she's so much like me. So much love to share. Her book will be a great success. All is well. Baby, don't worry about smoking. You will be fine, you will be a non-smoker soon. Love and Peace to all. Flobird.

GOLDENEAGLE

I have had dreams of her sitting on my shoulder whispering to me 'It's going to be OK,' and once on the beach near the Golden Gate Bridge, she walked across the water towards me.

MIKE

When M- got sober in September of 1979, Flobird spoke through him in her own voice while he was in a trance-like state and said, "We are in this world to love each other."

JOY

We enjoyed Flobird, but we did not feel connected to her as others did - different lifestyles, different needs. I feel she is at peace and is helping AIDS victims make the transition.

WAYNE

After my back operation, I couldn't walk. I had no control over my feet or my legs. When the doctors went in to operate, they found something was pushing against a nerve, so they had to pull the nerve out of the way, but it exploded inside. There was so much pressure and some trauma to the nerves, and it just happened to be the nerve to my leg. Before my operation, I couldn't even stand for more than a couple of minutes without tears in my eyes.

Afterwards I had to walk up and down this fence. I had to walk hand over hand, so I could walk up and down to try to strengthen that leg, and get that nerve back. Linda worked about two miles from where we lived, and I had been working out with this leg, and things seemed to be pretty good. I had decided I was going to take a walk down to Linda's place of work. I started down and cut across this field where a lot of construction was going on. I got to a point where the pain was just excruciating. I couldn't believe it. I had tears in my eyes, thinking, 'God, I can't go on, this is terrible.'

I saw these construction people, and I was going to ask them to call my wife and have her come get me, 'cause I was in such pain. As I was standing there resting for a minute, I glanced down. There was a feather laying on the ground right in front of me. It was kind of a long black feather with a lot of orange in it. I've never seen one like that since. I knew at that moment that Flobird was there saying, 'Keep on keepin' on.' At least that's what popped into my head when I picked up that feather.

I remember reaching down, picking it up thinking, 'Okay Flobird. Here we go. Keep on keepin' on. One foot in front of the other.' And I ended up making it. To this day, I believe if I'd stopped, that would have been the end of it. I'd have had real problems. But by that feather being there, and that saying, 'keep on keepin' on' going through my mind, I was able to keep walking.

So I know she's talked to me. In dreams ... there have been several dreams that Flobird has been in. But her presence is not something that's conscious all the time. It's something that's just there. Especially when I'm working with a newcomer. In that instance I can feel that feeling. They're coming at you, and they're saying all this horrible stuff, and you don't know what to say. All of a sudden, something clicks.

It's like I've said before, sometimes when I'm talking to people, I don't know what I'm saying. Words come out of my mouth, and I'm listening to myself and saying, 'Where in the Hell did that come from?' But if I listen close enough, it's the words that Flobird taught me. That's where they came from. Those same words came through Flobird. They were universal truths that came through her. I have picked them up and use them today.

I know that she's here. At times I can feel her. In the meetings sometimes when that newcomer is really hurting and really wants the Program, that feeling comes, chicken skin type thing, and there's that sense that she's there. Or when I'm talking to somebody who understands. Let's see, how can I put this. Somebody who knows more than the newcomer, as if I was talking to you, Cherie, and we were talking about spiritual things.

When I talk to Linda, I talk about Flobird quite a bit. We discuss her frequently. Things that she said in the past. Things I remember. And every time that happens, she's there. I know she's around. Her spirit comes down and touches me ever so often. What can I say. It's just part of my life.

I owe everything and anything because she was there and took the time to love me and care. Without that I'm sure I would have checked out, because I would have had to go back. It was too much for me. Life was just too bloody much for me. I was terrified of it. I was scared, and I'm still terrified and scared, but today I've got this inner strength and peace in me, and it was Flobird who was there to guide me to find my own Higher Power. She pointed the way out. She was like a path finder. She said, "Come on. You can do this. I've done this. Look at me. Don't be afraid. Follow your heart."

It's words like that which have allowed me to do so much in my life, in my work. It's every part of my being. I wish my kids could have met her. She was a tremendous influence on me. Everything I have is because of Flobird. She was there to lead me and point the way. I guess that's what I'm trying to say.

I think this book is very much needed. Things Flobird talked about, the metaphysics and stuff, taught me to follow my heart, and to trust my inner self. But the main thing she taught me was Love without a price tag. People need to understand. We don't need to get so deep into the metaphysics. We need to understand the love.

MARCHAND

If I could just give one quarter of love to everyone like she did, my life would be fulfilled. There's still a lot unsaid and yet it's all been said. Our feelings, our hopes and dreams, how do you put life, hope and all the love in the pages of a book? Maybe some lost souls will pick this up and hope will be born in their hearts because of all of our lives being bound together with our mother, our friend, spiritual advisor, and sponsor.

I still find many feathers on the ground in times of unknowing and in times of joy. I want to make a difference in people's lives and touch others as she did. She walks and talks with each of us in our hearts every day. We just have to be still and listen.

We all have scattered to different parts of the earth fulfilling our individual lives - learning, growing, reaching out to touch others. It's possible many would feel separated from each other, but when we see each other, it's as if no time has passed, and we share and care for each other as much or more than we ever did before. We all share a special camaraderie, a special portion of our hearts and lives with each other that will live forever.

Thank you, my beloved sister, for the opportunity to walk and talk and be a part of this work (Love made visible) of our dear mother. May all who participated within these pages, and all those that silently participated in her life and our lives know and feel they are blessed with our Father's divine love. Joy really is the most infallible sign of the presence of God. God bless us each and every one.

You must maintain peace, love, and joy. Start loving each other as God loves us. The revelations in the Bible...they are happening right now. The earthquakes, the tidal waves, the cosmic solar events are coming to our planet. This is why we've got to wake up. To wake up and help others.

-- Flobird

Beach Comers Group - 1974

Flobird - Big Island, Hawaii - 1970's

Flobird: A Bird's Eye View

Flobird - VA Beach - 1974

Flobird, Lorraine, Vivian

Flobird - VA Beach Country Club

Flobird - Midst Alcoholis - 1950's

Flobird - Years before stopped drinking - 1957

Flobird - Navy Dress - 1940's

Flobird: A Bird's Eye View

Flobird - Long Beach, CA - 1950's

High School Diploma

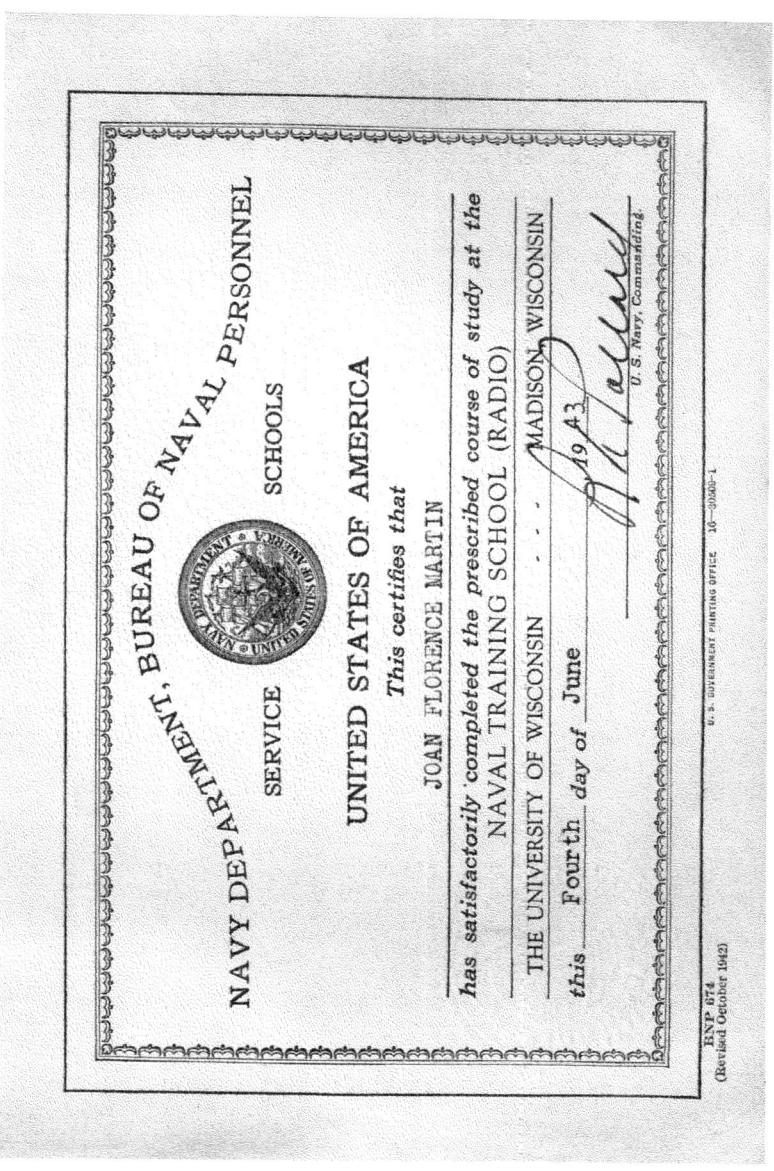

Naval Training School Document

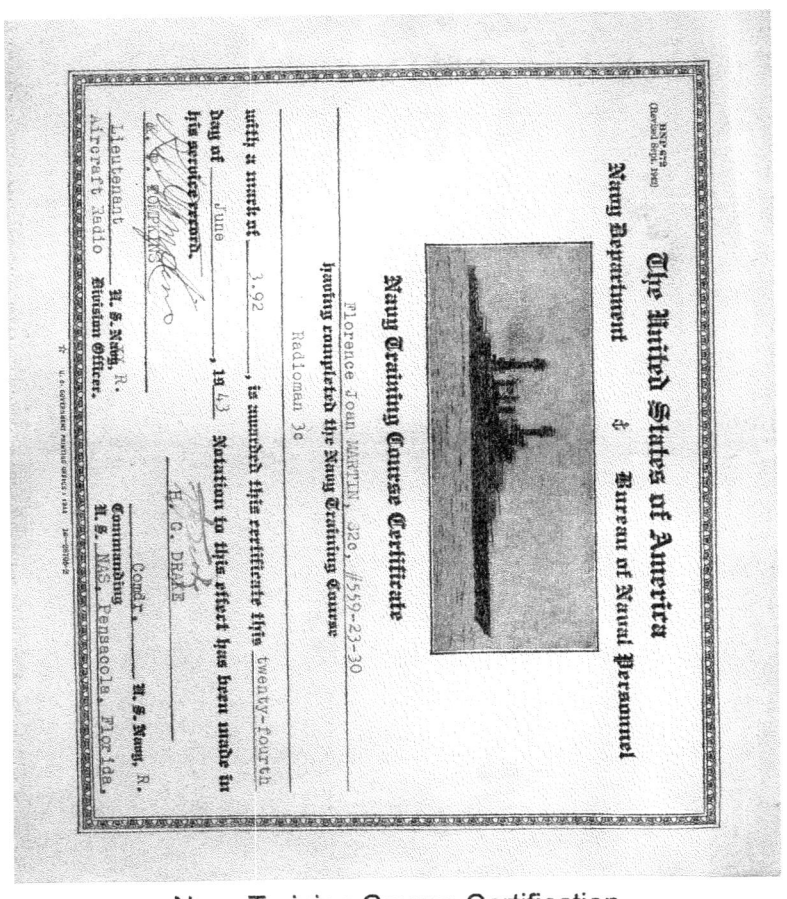

Navy Training Course Certification

To order this book, contact Cherie Johnson at:

dancedivaonline@yahoo.com

or write her at:

Hc2 Box 6848, Keaau, HI 96749

Please Call Anytime
Burl Haigwood
202-441-2400

GASOLINEGATE

BENZENE  ⚠ WARNING

BENZENE is a "Group A, known human carcinogen" – U.S. EPA
BENZENE is "Known to be a human carcinogen" – National Institutes of Health, Center for Disease Control and Prevention, Food and Drug Administration.
BENZENE is a "Carcinogenic to Humans" – World Health Organization.

CONTAINS UP TO 90% GASOLINE WITH BENZENE and/or
Toluene methyl**benzene**
Ethyl**benzene**
Xylene dimethyl**benzene**

Up to 10% of this Product Contains Ethanol which DOES NOT Contain Benzene

Why are you being warned about exposure to BENZENE?

☑ **BENZENE** exposure can cause leukemia.
☑ **BENZENE** can cause cancer and birth defects or other reproductive harm.
☑ **BENZENE** exposure during pregnancy may affect the development of the child. It may also harm the male reproductive system.
☑ **BENZENE** exposure warning labels are required by OHSA, DOT, and California Proposition 65 to be on products. Why are **BENZENE WARNING LABELS** not required on gasoline pumps?

#GASOLINEGATE

GASOLINEGATE
Burl Haigwood

Author
202.441.2400
gasolinegate@gmail.com

GASOLINEGATE [facebook]
@BURL_HAIGWOOD #GAS●LINEGATE [X]
BURL-HAIGWOOD [linkedin]
GASOLINEGATE.COM [web]

Please use the QR code to support the "I Give a Buck" education campaign by purchasing a Gasolinegate eBook for $1 on Amazon